# University of New Hampshire

Durham, New Hampshire

*Written by Jeff Lewis*
*Edited by Adam Burns*

*Additional contributions by Omid Gohari,*
*Christina Koshzow, Chris Mason, Kimberly Moore, Joey Rahimi,*
*Jon Skindzier, Luke Skurman, Tim Williams, Kevin Nash,*
*Justine Ezarik*

COLLEGE PROWLER

ISBN # 1-59658168-9
ISSN # 1552-1451
© Copyright 2005 College Prowler
All Rights Reserved
Printed in the U.S.A.
www.collegeprowler.com

**Special thanks to** Babs Carryer, Andy Hannah, LaunchCyte, Tim O'Brien, Bob Sehlinger, Thomas Emerson, Andrew Skurman, Barbara Skurman, Bert Mann, Dave Lehman, Daniel Fayock, Chris Babyak,The Donald H. Jones Center for Entrepreneurship, Terry Slease, Jerry McGinnis, Bill Ecenberger, Idie McGinty, Kyle Russell, Jacque Zaremba, Larry Winderbaum, Paul Kelly, Roland Allen, Jon Reider, Team Evankovich, Julie Fenstermaker, Lauren Varacalli, Abu Noaman, Jason Putorti, Mark Exler, Daniel Steinmeyer, Jared Cohon, Gabriela Oates, Tri Ad Litho, David Koegler, and Glen Meakem.

**Bounce Back Team:** Scott Mazuzan, Christopher Mongeon, and Adam Chouinard

College Prowler™
5001 Baum Blvd.
Suite 456
Pittsburgh, PA 15213

Phone: (412) 697-1390, 1(800) 290-2682
Fax: (412) 697-1396, 1(800) 772-4972
E-mail: info@collegeprowler.com
Website: www.collegeprowler.com

# Welcome to College Prowler™

During the writing of College Prowler's guidebooks, we felt it was critical that our content was unbiased and unaffiliated with any college or university. We think it's important that our readers get honest information and a realistic impression of the student opinions on any campus — that's why if any aspect of a particular school is terrible, we (unlike a campus brochure) intend to publish it. While we do keep an eye out for the occasional extremist — the cheerleader or the cynic — we take pride in letting the students tell it like it is. We strive to create a book that's as representative as possible of each particular campus. Our books cover both the good and the bad, and whether the survey responses point to recurring trends or a variation in opinion, these sentiments are directly and proportionally expressed through our guides.

College Prowler guidebooks are in the hands of students throughout the entire process of their creation. Because you can't make student-written guides without the students, we have students at each campus who help write, randomly survey their peers, edit, layout, and perform accuracy checks on every book that we publish. From the very beginning, student writers gather the most up-to-date stats, facts, and inside information on their colleges. They fill each section with student quotes and summarize the findings in editorial reviews. In addition, each school receives a collection of letter grades (A through F) that reflect student opinion and help to represent contentment, prominence, or satisfaction for each of our 20 specific categories. Just as in grade school, the higher the mark the more content, more prominent, or more satisfied the students are with the particular category.

Once a book is written, additional students serve as editors and check for accuracy even more extensively. Our bounce-back team — a group of randomly selected students who have no involvement with the project — are asked to read over the material in order to help ensure that the book accurately expresses every aspect of the university and its students. This same process is applied to the 200-plus schools College Prowler currently covers. Each book is the result of endless student contributions, hundreds of pages of research and writing, and countless hours of hard work. All of this has led to the creation of a student information network that stretches across the nation to every school that we cover. It's no easy accomplishment, but it's the reason that our guides are such a great resource.

When reading our books and looking at our grades, keep in mind that every college is different and that the students who make up each school are not uniform — as a result, it is important to assess schools on a case-by-case basis. Because it's impossible to summarize an entire school with a single number or description, each book provides a dialogue, not a decision, that's made up of 20 different topics and hundreds of student quotes. In the end, we hope that this guide will serve as a valuable tool in your college selection process. Enjoy!

OMID GOHARI ◯ CHRISTINA KOSHZOW ◯ CHRIS MASON ◯ JOEY RAHIMI ◯ LUKE SKURMAN ◯
*The College Prowler™ Team*

## UNIVERSITY OF NEW HAMPSHIRE
# Table of Contents

# Introduction from the Author

Welcome to UNH. As you cruise down the highway you may notice the houses and towns beginning to disappear. Don't worry though; you are in the right place. Eventually the town of Durham springs from the horizon. This vintage campus is quite a sight among the farms and hayfields that surround it. The town is one of the smallest in New Hampshire, but during the school year it swells with approximately 12,000 students.

The students are a very mixed breed. There are people that come from as far away as India and there are some who commute from the house down the street. There are the typical athletes, Greek students, multicultural students, all-American students and the "average Joes". There is a friend for everyone

There is also a major for everyone. The campus offers everything from business, environmental studies, liberal arts, studio arts, sciences and much more. UNH is most well known for its studies in Science, Business and it is one of the few Agricultural schools left in the nation. The majority of teachers at UNH are there for research and that often affects the availability of some teachers, but they all genuinely care for the progress of the students, and are more than willing to help those who want it.

Athletically, UNH is a Division I school. The only team that gets most of the spotlight is Hockey though, and they deserve it. The rest of the athletic programs at UNH are decent. So if you are not a hockey fan, then there are plenty of other things to do.

For those interested in UNH. The best thing you can do is come and visit. The tour guides are helpful and take their job very seriously. You will probably want to visit a couple of times: once during the winter and in springtime. This way you will be able to fully experience the atmosphere of UNH. Another good thing to do is sit in on a couple classes, which teachers are more than willing to accommodate. I think the best thing about UNH is its ability to appeal to many different personalities. Generally, the school has a very unique ability to grow on people, so the best advice is to just give it a chance.

Jeff Lewis, Author
University of New Hampshire

# By the Numbers

## General Information

University of New Hampshire
155, Durham, NH
Durham, NH 03824

**Control:**
Public

**Academic Calendar:**
Semester

**Religious Affiliation:**
None

**Founded:**
1866

**Website:**
www.unh.edu

**Main Phone:**
862-1360

**Admissions Phone:**
862-1360

## Student Body

**Full-Time
Undergraduates:**
10,700

**Part Time Undergraduates:**
816

**Total Males:**
4,977

**Total Female:**
6,539

**Male to Female Ratio:**
43% to 57%

# Admissions

**Overall Acceptance Rate:**
69%

**Early Decision Acceptance Rate:**
63%

**Total Applicants:**
10,798

**Total Acceptances:**
7,502

**Freshman Enrollment:**
2,452

**Yield
(% Of Admitted Students Who Actually Enroll):**
33%

**Early Decision Available?**
No

**Early Action Available?**
Yes

**Early Action Deadline:**
Dec 1

**Early Action Notification:**
Jan 15

**Regular Decision Deadline:**
Feb 1

**Regular Decision Notification:**
Apr 15

**Must Reply-By Date:**
May 1

**Common Application Accepted?**
Yes

**Supplemental Forms?**
No

**Admissions Phone:**
862-1360

**Admissions E-mail:**
admissions@unh.edu

**Admissions Website:**
www.unh.edu/admissions

**SAT I or ACT Required?**
SAT required

**SAT I Range
(25th - 75th Percentile):**
1010 – 1230

**SAT I Verbal Range
(25th – 75th Percentile):**
1010 – 1230

**SAT I Math Range
(25th – 75th Percentile):**
510 - 620

**Retention Rate:**
85%

**Top 10% of
High School lass:**
20%

**Application Fee:**
$45

**Applicants Placed on Waiting List:**
200

**Applicants Accepted from Waiting List:**
137

**Students Enrolled from Waiting List:**
1137

**Transfer Applications Received:**
1158

**Transfer Applications Accepted:**
700

**Transfer Students Enrolled:**
383

**Transfer Applicant Acceptance Rate:**
68%

# Financial Information

**In State Tuition:**
$9,226

**Out of State:**
$20,256

**Room and Board:**
$6,612

**Books and Supplies:**
$1,100

**Average Need-Based Financial Aid Package:**
$14,267
(including loans, work-study, grants, and other sources)

**Students Who Applied For Financial Aid:**
68%

**Students Who Received Aid:**
56%

**Financial Aid Forms Deadline:**
Mar 1

**Financial Aid Phone:**
862-3600

**Financial Aid Email:**
Financial.Aid@unh.edu

**Financial Aid Website:**
www.unh.edu./financial-aid/index.html

# Academics

The Lowdown On...
## Academics

**Degrees Awarded:**
Associate
Bachelor's
Master's
Post-master's certificate
Doctorate

**Most Popular Areas of Study:**
Business  15%
Social Sciences  15%
Health Professions  10%
English  7%

**Undergraduate Schools:**
College of Engineering and Physical Sciences
College of Liberal Arts
College of Life Sciences and Agriculture
School of Health and Human Services
Thompson School of Applied Sciences
Whittemore School of Business and Economics

**Full-Time Faculty:**
588

## Faculty with Terminal Degree:
92%

## Student-to-Faculty Ratio:
14 to 1

## Average Course Load:
4

## Best Places to Study:
Dimond Library
Memorial Union Building

## Sample Academic Clubs:
American Sign Language Club
Earth Science Club
Mock Trial Club
National Society of Minorities in Hospitality
Society of Woman Engineers

## Special Study Options
Cross-registration
Double major
English as a second language (esl)
Exchange student program (domestic)
Honors program
Independent study
Internships
Student-designed major
Study abroad
Teacher certificate program

## AP Test Score Requirements:
Possible credit for scores of 3,4 or 5

## IB Test Score Requirements:
Possible credit for scores of 5, 6, 7 (on a higher level)

## Did You Know?

The University's international research opportunities program (IROP) was the first of its kind. It serves as a model for others nationwide.

UNH ranks in the top thirty educational institutions nationwide, and the top two in New England, in funding from the National Aeronautics and Space Administration (NASA).

The Institute for Scientific Information named UNH among a handful of "influential" universities that included Harvard, Columbia, Stanford, and Carnegie Mellon.

## Students Speak Out On...
# Academics

"It depends on your classes and what you like in a teacher. At the end of the semester we fill out evaluations, which you can access in the library to find out about teachers before you enroll in their classes."

Q "The teachers are very helpful, outgoing professionals-that **truly care about the student's experience.**"

Q "Some teachers can be very good, and some tend to be **rather boring and unprofessional.** The same goes for classes."

Q "Most of the teachers try and **make themselves available** to students, by making office hours. If you can't make it to their office hours they're usually good about making an appointment to see you. Yes, all of the classes I have taken (with the exception of Economics and Propaganda) have been extremely interesting."

Q "My teachers have ranged from boring to interesting, passionate to blithering, but for the most part have all been **knowledgeable and concerned about my education.**"

Q "The teachers are interested in what they are teaching and in the students. **I find most of my classes interesting.**"

Q "Teachers are usually pretty friendly and some **seem more involved with their research** at UNH than their classes. Most of my classes are interesting."

Q "From what I've heard, it varies from department to department, but all of the teachers that I have had are wonderful. Obviously, **teaching methods vary and some are more effective** to me than others, but teachers are always available during office hours or by appointment to help you. Also, in a lot of cases, there are teaching assistants around. Contrary to popular belief, the professors and TAs really do want to see you succeed."

Q "Some are the best I've ever had; some are the worst. There are always **study groups and lots of support** from the Center for Academic Research (CFAR), if you're having trouble. CFAR is great, and there you can read comments from students about teachers, if you want to know who to look out for."

Q "The teachers are good but they can be **hard depending on your major.**"

Q "It depends on what you take, but I've only had one teacher who really stunk. Most professors are **helpful and try to understand their students' needs**, but they can also be frustrating."

Q "Get to know your teachers and they will definitely help you out in the future. Even though it's a big school, the **large classes can feel small** when you get to know the professor and some of the other students."

# The College Prowler Take On...
# Academics

Every student has their favorite teacher and their most despised teacher. Most students at UNH agree that the teachers that are good at their job make up for the others. Although a large percentage of teachers at UNH are also doing research, and may not have as much time for students, they still seem to have a lot of compassion for the students and are always willing to help students who really want it and need it. All UNH teachers post office hours and devoutly stick to them in order for their students to have access to them pretty much any hour of the daytime. If a teachers' office hours coincide with your daily schedule appointments are available.

At every college there are classes that you may not like very much. With all the course requirements given out today (at all national universities) it is a given that you'll probably have to take classes that you have little or no interest in. UNH is no different. The lecture classes tend to range in the hundreds and every student has a set of general education requirements to reach before graduation. The Center for Academic Research (CFAR) is more than willing to give advice on what courses and professors to take, and can even show you student quotes and opinions (much like the quotes in this guidebook) that will give you a better idea of what direction you want to go. On the occasion you do have to take a large lecture class, there are plenty of options to choose something interesting. Also, professors always have teaching assistants on hand who are more than willing to help.

**B-**

The College Prowler™ Grade on
Academics: B-

A high Academics grade generally indicates that professors are knowledgeable, accessible, and genuinely interested in their students' welfare.

# Local Atmosphere

**The Lowdown On...**
## Local Atmosphere

**Region:**
Northeast

**City, State:**
Durham, NH

**Setting:**
Rural

**Distance from Portsmouth:**
10 minutes

**Distance from Boston:**
45 minutes

**Points of Interest:**
NH seacoast

**Closest Shopping Malls:**
Fox Run Mall (Newington, NH)

➜

## Closest Movie Theatres:

Regal Newington 12
45 Gosling Road, Newington, NH 03801.
Movieline: 603-431-6116

Portsmouth 5
581 Lafayette Road, Portsmouth, NH 03801.
Movieline: 603-436-9281

## Major Sports Teams:

Boston Bruins
Boston Celtics
New England Patriots
New England Revolution (soccer)
Boston Red Sox

## City Websites:

www.ci.durham.nh.us

## Did You Know?

### Five Fun Facts about Durham:

- Major General John Sullivan was a resident of Durham New Hampshire. He left the Continental Congress to serve under Washington from Cambridge to Valley Forge. Commanded at Rhode Island in 1778, and led campaign against the Six Nations in New York in 1779. Sullivan re-entered Congress, then served three times as Governor of New Hampshire. Sullivan then led the fight for ratification of U.S. Constitution and became a federal district judge.

- July 18, 1694, a force of about 250 Indians under command of the French soldier, de Villies, attacked settlements in the Durham area on both sides of the Oyster River, killing or capturing approximately 100 settlers, it was the most devastating raid in New Hampshire during the French and Indian War.

→

- Make sure to visit Adams Point, a beautiful estuary located on Great Bay, where families and hikers bring picnic baskets and binoculars to spend a day enjoying the scenery, catching glimpses of wildlife.
- Durham is only fifteen minutes from miles of seacoast beaches.
- UNH owns 2,600 acres of land around Durham that is used for walking, biking, and skiing trails for students.

## Famous People From...

Durham: John Sullivan (1st governor of NH)

Hampton: Eunice "Goody" Cole (the only woman to be convicted of witchcraft)

Portsmouth: Celia Thaxter (poet)

Dover: Jenny Thompson (Olympic swimmer)

## Local Slang:

**Wicked -** replaces the intensive "very". For example: "It's wicked cold outside."

**Blinker -** The directional light on your car.

**Nor'easter -** A storm that moves from the north-east and brings those "wicked" bad storms.

## Students Speak Out On...
# Local Atmosphere

"Newington and Portsmouth are ten minutes away, with nice restaurants and theaters. If you're in the mood for some sun, the ocean is only twenty minutes from campus."

Q "The town is **small but quaint,** with a great college atmosphere."

Q "Durham is an awesome little town with a **lot of stuff to check out.**"

Q "Durham is your typical small town. There is a quaint downtown area with a few shops and restaurants, but other than that, the **university really makes the town.**"

Q "The town is almost exclusively centered around the college. There are no other universities in town. It is a very small town with **not much to do in Durham.**"

Q "Durham is a cool little town, and good shops and restaurants aren't that far away at all, **Pauly's Pockets in downtown Durham is awesome.**"

Q "There are no other universities here. Durham is a **one street town.**"

Q "The town is pretty accepting of the college because **we give the shops and restaurants most of their business.** There are no nearby colleges and there's nothing too exciting going on in town."

Q "There are no other universities in the area. The town we are in is very quaint and quiet. It's a **great town if you're an earthy type of person**. There are many outdoor activities available. There really isn't anything in the area to stay away from, although there are many pretty things, like the waterfall on the path in the college woods."

Q "I love Durham! UNH is a big school in a quaint town. Downtown Durham runs right through the campus, so you see students sitting outside coffee shops or just hanging out at the restaurants all the time. New Hampshire is really beautiful, and **there are a lot of things to do** in the area."

Q "When it's nice out, the school sometimes has **big barbeques where you can eat all you want for free.** I thought that was cool when I first got here. It's a great campus. Everything is in walking distance, and the historic buildings make it so pretty."

Q "Durham is great and so is Portsmouth, which is nearby. I plan on moving there eventually. It's just beautiful. The atmosphere at **UNH makes you want to have a good time.**"

# The College Prowler Take On...
## Local Atmosphere

Durham, NH is the ideal hometown for The University of New Hampshire. It is probably safe to say that the two are co-dependent of one another. The students, all but unanimously, love everything about the town, while many Durham shops stay in business because of UNH students. The rural atmosphere also makes for a comfortable and serene learning environment. Durham itself inhabits a collection of small suburbs close to the campus and there are vast farming fields surrounding it all.  There is a definite distinction between the college students and the so called locals.  Durham, like any other small town, has a high school and elementary school, a post office, numerous gas stations, a few casual bars where the locals and students often mingle, and a small shopping plaza for all the necessities.  All of these attractions are tightly lined up along a single main street that passes through the campus.  The night life solely belongs to the students. If it weren't for the campus, Durham would probably be boring, to say the least.

Durham is probably one of the smallest towns in New Hampshire, and when you stick more than 12,000 students in the middle of it you get an interesting mix of relaxed locals and wild college students. The town does seem to rub off on the students though. You can always find students relaxing downtown on a nice day. Durham is an incredibly friendly town. Most of the residents are students, or those who have learned to accept the students as a part of their community.

**B**

The College Prowler™ Grade on

Local
Atmosphere: B

A high Local Atmosphere grade indicates that the area surrounding campus is safe and scenic. Other factors include nearby attractions, proximity to other schools, and the town's attitude toward students

# Safety & Security

**The Lowdown On...**
## Safety & Security

**Number of UNH Police:**
15

**UNH Police Phone:**
862-1427

**Safety Services:**
Security Escort Service
SAFE Rides
Fire Safety
Sexual Harassment and
Rape Prevention Program(S.
H.A.R.P.P.)

**Health Services:**
Basic medical services
On-site pharmaceuticals
STD screening
Counseling and psychological
services
Acupuncture
Allergy/immunization
Massage therapy/meditation/
yoga
Student-run help line

→

## Health Center Office Hours:

Health Center Office Hours:
Monday, Tuesday, Thursday, Friday:
7:30 a.m. - 4:30 p.m.
Wednesday:
7:30 a.m. - 7:30 p.m.

Saturday and Sunday:
12 noon - 4 p.m.
Labor Day, Veteran's Day & Martin Luther King Day:
12 noon - 4 p.m.
Summer and Semester Breaks, M - F:
8 a.m. - 4:30 p.m.

## Did You Know?

UNH Campus Police provide vehicle jump-starts with a special "Jump Pack" that looks like something straight out of Ghostbusters!

## Students Speak Out On...
# Safety & Security

"The security system is pretty good. There are safety lights and emergency call boxes at regular intervals and campus security patrols the campus."

Q "I feel very safe on campus, although **security is a bit overwhelming** at times."

Q "Security is really, really awesome actually. **I have never once felt unsafe.**"

Q "I don't know a lot about campus security, because it has never really been an issue (which I guess is a good thing). UNH is a place where walking around at night could be potentially scary, because there are not a lot of people out, and there are a lot of wooded paths. But there are **lights with emergency call boxes and panic buttons** that can be seen from all over, and you really just get a sense of security on campus."

Q "Security is good. There are **twenty-four hour lock-downs in residence halls,** two full size police forces at all times, two minute response time at emergency call boxes, student security officers, bike cops, and more."

Q "There have been **incidents of peeping toms** before on campus, but most problems have been resolved. We have security call boxes around campus, which makes me feel safer."

Q "Campus and Durham Police are always out and are actually so pervasive that students get mad at them. They are there, however, and **they look out for us.**"

Q "Security at UNH is extreme. It's a safe environment, and I feel fine walking from one dorm to another at night or in the afternoon. You can always **call for a free escort if you feel unsafe."**

Q "There are **a lot of police on the weekends.** We have the university police, the Durham police, usually some state troopers, and on busy weekends, police will come in from surrounding towns to help out. Located throughout the campus are little booths where you can call the police by just pressing a button. I feel fairly safe at night, but it is always a good idea to go out in groups of people. As long as you stay on the main roads and off of the trails at night, you should be all right."

Q "UNH takes safety and security very seriously. **Each student must use an ID to get into his or her dorm** at night time. It's very reassuring. There are many student activist groups that make safety a priority, like S.H.A.R.P.P., which is our rape prevention center. The campus also has emergency call boxes all over campus, identified by a glowing blue light on top for use in emergency situations."

Q "At first I was hesitant, just because I was brought up being cautious of everything, but it is very safe. The majority of the town population is the students, so **everyone watches out for everyone else**, though you still need to be careful."

Q "Security is a lot better now than it was when I began here five years ago. **They have really cracked down in the dorms**, but it is just like any other college."

# The College Prowler Take On...
## Safety & Security

Since UNH is a small campus it is much easier to keep safe. However, no place (not even Durham) is ultimately safe. Most recently, the campus has dealt with a couple stalking cases, and overall there haven't been any serious problems. It would be illogical to let a few isolated cases deter from how safe Durham really is. The campus police have a great relationship with the students and greatly care about their safety. When the safety of the students is compromised, the students are never left in the dark. Logistically, the emergency lights have a call button and an alarm that links them directly to the headquarters of campus security. In theory, the lights are also placed so that each one can be seen from another light so that if someone is running from a threat they can be tracked and helped more efficiently. With the recent problems with terrorism, all dormitories have been locked down twenty-four hours a day and seven days a week.

The local Durham Ambulance Corps also helps with the safety of the students and community. On call twenty-four hours a day and seven days a week, these highly trained individuals tend to any problems that students may have. They spend most of their time responding to parties where people have drank too much, but they have seen every kind of emergency at least twice. Overall, the campus is fairly safe and most students probably don't think twice about a walk alone to their car at night.

**A**

The College Prowler™ Grade on

Safety &
Security: A

A high grade in Safety & Security means that students generally feel safe, campus police are visible, bluelight phones and escort services are readily available, and safety precautions are not overly necessary.

# Computers

### The Lowdown On...
## Computers

**High-Speed Network?**
Yes.

**Wireless Network?**
Yes

**Number of Labs:**
7

**Number of Computers:**
208

**Operating Systems:**
Windows(157 computers),
Macintosh(51 computers)

Linux(16 computers)

## Free Software:

Adobe Acrobat 5.0
Adobe Acrobat Reader 5.1
Adobe Photoshop 7.0
McAfee VirusScan 4.5
Microsoft Access 2000
Microsoft PowerPoint 2000
Microsoft Word X
Matlab 6.5 R13
WS-FTP95 LE
Mozilla 1.2
AppleWorks 6.2.4.

## 24-Hour Labs:

McConnell 104
Kingsbury 128
Kingsbury 317 (Unix)

## Charge to Print?

Yes

## Did You Know?

235,345 students log onto campus computers each year

## Students Speak Out On...
# Computers

> "The network is good. The labs are usually crowded, but there are so many on campus that you can usually find at least one."

Q "I don't know anybody who doesn't have their own computer, so I would definitely recommend it. The network is great, and **every student has their own high speed internet connection**, and there are multiple clusters across campus where students can use facilities if it is more convenient for them."

Q "I would **recommend bringing a personal computer.** I have not used any of the computer clusters on-campus."

Q "We have **seven on-campus computer clusters**, and one is open twenty-four hours a day. If you don't have your own computer you will never have a hard time finding one. The library also rents out laptops. Most people do bring their own computer though. Each resident in a dorm gets their own high speed internet connection."

Q "Computers that allow printing are always crowded, we get fast internet connection though, and **you can check out laptops in the library** to use."

Q "I would definitely bring your own computer. It's a hassle to haul all your schoolwork to the clusters. The clusters are never full, and there is always a free computer on campus. There is one computer cluster that is open twenty-four hours a day which is helpful. The clusters have **both Macs and PCs,** which is a plus. The computer network in the dorms is very fast. I am very satisfied with our networking on campus."

Q "I would recommend bringing your own computer, as there are only two labs open twenty-four hours. They get **very crowded around midterms and finals,** and it is nearly impossible to get in."

Q "Bringing your own computer is a good idea-you'll find you use it a lot. The internet connection is great-it's fast, and you can be online all the time. You'll find **AIM is big around here**. It's the way to talk and much easier than the phone for talking to buddies on or off-campus."

Q "The labs are not always crowded, but you can always work around that. Just don't wait until the last minute to do your assignments if you don't have a computer. I would **bring your computer.** People are constantly signed on Instant Messenger. IM is your lifeblood at school."

Q "If you want to bring a computer and your only choice is an old one with old programs, don't bother. **UNH uses all the newest programs,** and all the professors will ask you to use them as well."

# The College Prowler Take On...
# Computers

Although the number of labs might be a bit small for the amount of people at UNH, there is always at least one open. Most of the students bring their own computer just because it makes their life easier in the end. College is not completely impossible without a computer though. UNH tries very hard to keep their computer programs updated. Also, the student network is fast and efficient and very rarely malfunctions or shuts down completely. I've heard horror stories of similar occurrences at other schools (during finals week no less). All UNH labs are updated with the newest PCs (Dell, Compaq, Macintosh) and are available to all UNH students. So, even if you don't have the convenience of your own personal computer, the ones provided for you are more than adequate.

The campus has many options for renting laptops or purchasing software from a very good computer store on campus. The campus computer store also repairs student computers for good prices.  UNH has a T3 cable connection to all the dorms, the library and other computer labs. People with wireless laptops can also get internet connections in the library. Overall, the computers available on campus are top-of-the-line and the services the campus offers are very helpful.

**B-**

The College Prowler™ Grade on
## Computers: B-

A high grade in Computers designates that computer labs are available, the computer network is easily accessible, and the campus' computing technology is up-to-date.

# Facilities

The Lowdown On...
## Facilities

**Campus Size:**
2,600 acres

**Libraries:**
2

**Student Center:**
The Memorial Union Building

**Athletic Center:**
The Whittemore Center/Hamel
Recreation Center

The field house

## What Is There to Do On Campus?

The campus offers many activities including billiards, swimming classes and activities, working out at the gym, dining from 730 a.m. -930 p.m., or attending scheduled entertainment in the Memorial Union Building (MUB)

## Popular Places to Chill:

The most popular places are on Main Street, where on a warm day you can find students relaxing outside of Murphy's Tin Palace or Breaking New Grounds on the patio seats.

Another popular place is the Thompson Hall lawn which is ideal for throwing a frisbee or just lounging around.

## Favorite Things to Do:

If you're looking to kill a few minutes between classes you can find plenty do in the Memorial Union Building, such as studying with a fresh coffee, or milkshake. There is a large billiards room on the ground floor where you can always find a table. If you have more time on your hands, the MUB has events scheduled every day including a lecture series, musical performances, comedians, and club meetings.

## Movie Theatre on Campus?

There are two movie theater auditoriums in the Memorial Union Building

## Bowling on Campus?

No.

## Bar on Campus?

On Main Street there is Murphy's Tin Palace, Scorpions, and Libby's Bar and restaurant

## Coffeehouse on Campus?

In the Memorial Union Building there is the Panache Café, an on main street the local favorite is Breaking New Grounds (BNG)

## Students Speak Out On...
# Facilities

"UNH has a wonderful gym that offers aerobics, workout facilities, an indoor tack, racquet ball, saunas, and basket ball. The student center is pretty big and is a nice place to go for dinner, too."

Q "The facilities are all pretty nice. UNH is in the process of building a new dorm and dining hall, which will be awesome! **The gym on campus is really amazing**-it's packed at times, but we have a lot of kids here. We have an indoor track, and the gym equipment is pretty much all new. The computer centers are located all over campus and are really nice. If there is anything you need, there are different places to help you in the Student Center. The people are really nice and offer to help with everything."

Q "The gym is great, but **always crowded**. The athletic facilities are well-maintained."

Q "All of our facilities are very nice. The student center doesn't have a ton in it, but it's got the typical pool tables and living rooms that students need. Our athletic facilities are beautiful. So beautiful, in fact, that **the gym is always crowded.**"

Q "UNH just built **an awesome new workout facility**. It's free to all students-a lot of schools don't have that perk. Most of the buildings are pretty new and very clean, with new equipment. Some lecture halls are old, but still nice."

Q "The campus facilities are top-notch. The MUB is **a great place to hang out** and there is a multitude of things to do there, from movies to coffee. The athletic facilities are also very nice and offer a wide range of exercise programs."

Q "The student athletic center is very nice and popular (good equipment and facilities). The computers are also pretty new. The student center (MUB) is **a great building with a ton of different things to do.** There are movie theatres, retail food operations, the mail room, meeting rooms/lounges, student activity offices. The list goes on and on. It is also a beautiful building."

Q **"Facilities here are very nice.** They could use a bigger gym though because it's always packed. Some of the dorms and class buildings seem outdated."

Q "The facilities on campus are top-of-the-line. The new dining hall has really good food, and a nice atmosphere. There is the MUB, which is basically the student union, which is nice and has many things to do in it. The on-campus gym is really nice. They're always adding new equipment to it. The gym is air conditioned, too, which is a plus. We also have an indoor ice rink for ice skating and activities during the winter. We have **a year-round indoor pool**. We also have basketball and tennis courts to use."

Q "The gym (Whittemore Center) is awesome. **It has to be nice, since we are Division I** in sports. The student center has really good food. Sometimes I sit and do my work there because you see everyone you know."

Q "The gym is nice but always busy. The school is quickly outgrowing the new facility. The Library was brand new my freshman year and is **a great place to study or take a nap."**

# The College Prowler Take On...
# Facilities

The UNH campus offers a lot to its students. They have recently renovated the athletic centers, library, and numerous dorms. This year the campus opened the new $26 million dollar dining hall Holloway Commons, and the new dorm Mills Hall. Mills Hall is a suite dorm with five to eight person rooms with deluxe bathrooms and a living room in each.

UNH has many fields and two main athletic centers to accommodate the Division I sports teams on campus. Mostly due to the strength of the UNH hockey team, a prime ice-skating rink, open to all students, is located on campus. The rink can get a bit crowded, especially on the weekends. Most times, all the athletic facilities can be a bit crowded due to increasing student enrollment each year. There are ways around this though. Going to the gym early in the morning, or late at night, will greatly increase your chances of getting on the exercise machines that you want to use. Also, UNH has plans for more renovations in all its dorms. A multi-story parking garage may also be on the agenda of the campus administration in the near future. However, until more space is available, most students work around the crowded times at the gym, or the pool. Overall, the students at UNH seem generally happy with the facilities provided for them.

**B+**

The College Prowler™ Grade on
Facilities: B+

A high Facilities grade indicates that the campus is aesthetically pleasing and well-maintained; facilities are state-of-the-art, and libraries are exceptional. Other determining factors include the quality of both athletic and student centers and an abundance of things to do on campus.

# Campus Dining

**The Lowdown On...**
## Campus Dining

### Freshman Meal Plan Requirement?
No

### Meal Plan Average Cost:
$1,123 - $1,165

### Places to Grab a Bite with Your Meal Plan

**Holloway Commons**
Location: Memorial Union Building
Food:  Everything
Favorite Dish: Bread Sticks
Hours: Mon-Fri 7:15 a.m.-9:30 p.m.
Weekends 10 a.m. to 9:30 p.m.

### Panache Café

Location: Memorial Union Building

Food: beverages, sandwiches, salads, breakfast

Favorite Dish: New England Clam Chowder

Hours: Mon-Fri 7:30 a.m. to 1 a.m.

Weekends 11 a.m. to 1 a.m.

### Stillings Dining Hall

Location: Area 1 behind Stoke Hall Dorm

Food: Everything

Favorite Dish: Grilled Cheese

Hours: Mon-Fri 7:15 a.m.-7:30 p.m.

Weekends Closed

### Philbrook Dining Hall

Location: Area 3 between Williamson and Christiansen Dorms

Food: Everything

Favorite Dish: Chicken nuggets

Hours: Mon-Fri 7:15 a.m.-7:30 p.m.

Weekends Closed

## Off-Campus Places to Use Your Meal Plan:

None.

## Student Favorites:

Holloway Commons and Campus Convenience

## Other Options:

Kurt's Lunch Box, It's a Wrap (food trucks)

## 24-Hour On-Campus Eating?

Campus Convenience and Store 24

## Did You Know?

The university's new dining hall, Holloway Commons cost about $26 million to get up and running.

## Students Speak Out On...
# Campus Dining

> **"The campus food itself is really good, but Holloway Commons (the main dining hall) can be a bit frustrating at times."**

Q "The food is not that great, but there are a lot of places around campus that are good to eat. There is a commons building in the center of campus known as the MUB, and there all kinds of places to eat there, such as Taco Bell and D'Angelos. There are **all kinds of healthy things** to eat, if that is something you like."

Q "The dining halls are not that great, but they are definitely **a step up from high school cuisine.**"

Q "The food is sometimes awesome, and sometimes just good. I guess it **depends on your taste buds.**"

Q "Compared to most schools (so I've heard), our dining halls are pretty good. We have **unlimited meal plans and a wide variety of foods** at the dining hall. In addition to whatever the main course is for the night, we always have pizza, stir fry, salad bars, sandwich bars, soups, grilled food, and many other things to choose from. I eat a lot better at school than at home. Besides the three dining halls, we have a couple of cafe-like places where you can buy food to take out with you. It's convenient for people who are always going to and from classes."

Q "The dining halls are alright, but **they get old quickly.**"

Q "Any dining hall pretty much stinks. They have their good days, bu**t they're not too great overall.** On campus, Joe's Pizza is always popular for party nights. Domino's, JP's Subs and Durham House of Pizza are all pretty good, and Stat's has awesome ice cream."

Q "The food here is awesome. Our **dining services program has a great reputation."**

Q "Food is a lot better than other campuses and **they actually have vegan options,** but they still need some work. People love to get dollar slice pizza downtown, and Pauly's makes awesome falafel."

Q "The dining halls suck, but I'm sure that is the same everywhere. On campus there isn't really too much, besides some pizza places and a restaurant called Benjamin's, where they have good food. My favorite place to eat is the MUB (Memorial Union Building), where they have a **food court with Chinese food, pizza, sandwiches, Taco Bell,** and other foods like that."

Q "The dining halls are surprisingly not bad. **We just got a new dining hall** which I enjoy a lot. The MUB has a food court in it that has many places to go. There is a sub shop, a burger place, a taco bell, a Chinese food stop, and a counter for vegetarian fare."

Q "We all complain about the food at UNH, but the school has won many awards for the food. It's actually very good. People complain because, like any other school, it can get old. The good thing is that if you don't always want to go to the dining hall, the MUB has good food and you can use your meal plan there. **You can also use 'Cats Cache' at most downtown restaurants,** so there are many options."

# The College Prowler Take On...
# Campus Dining

UNH Dining Services tries very hard to please as many students as they can, and they have won numerous awards for their efforts. The students who complain about the UNH campus food selection must realize that dining hall food has to be produced in mass quantity. In the process of making large amounts of food, many of it may lose some of its flavor, hence the awful reputation that dining hall food has universally received. Students should, however, have a say in how they want their food prepared. This leads us to the most interesting thing about UNH dining, the "napkin notes." Students are encouraged to write suggestions and comments on their napkins and place them in a special box located at the exit of the three main campus dining halls (Panache Café excluded). Every napkin note is read and responded to via a napkin note board that is placed in the entrance of every dining hall. Many of the students concerns and wishes have been accommodated in this way.

While the food can get old on campus, Dining Services also has a "Cats Cache" program that allows students to put money on their student ID card, which can, in turn, be used at certain shops downtown to purchase not only food but many other items. This adds a little variety and excitement to the UNH students' dining options considering that students aren't limited to campus grounds when their stomachs start rumbling. Overall, the campus food services genuinely go out of the way to please the students in any way they can.

**The College Prowler™ Grade on**
**Campus Dining: B**

Our grade on Campus Dining addresses the quality of both school-owned dining halls and independent on-campus restaurants as well as the price, availability, and variety of food.

# Off-Campus Dining

The Lowdown On...
## Off-Campus Dining

### Restaurant Prowler:
## Popular Places to Eat!

**Durham House of Pizza**
Food: pizza and subs
Address:  42 Main St.
Durham, NH
Phone: 868-2224
Cool Features:  $1 pizza after 11pm on weekends
Price: $10 and under per person
Hours: Sunday - Wednesday 11 a.m. - 11 p.m.
Thursday - Saturday 11 a.m. - 2 a.m.

**The Bagelry**
Food: bagels and sandwiches
Address:  1 Mill Road
Plaza Durham, NH
Phone: 868-3500
Price: $10 and under per person
Hours: Sunday - Wednesday 6 a.m. - 5 p.m.
Thursday - Saturday 6 a.m. - 7 p.m.

**Breaking New Grounds**
Food: Coffee Shop
Address:  50B Main St.
Durham, NH
Phone: 868-6869

→

Price: $5 and under per person

Hours: Monday - Thursday 6:30 a.m. - 11:30 p.m.

Friday - Saturday 6:30 a.m. - 10 p.m.

### Domino's Pizza

Food: Pizza

Address: Mill Road Plaza

Durham, NH

Phone: 868-6230

Price: $10 and under per person

Hours: Monday - Sunday 10 a.m. - 4 a.m.

### Joe's NY Style Pizza

Food: Pizza

Address: 41 Main St.

Durham, NH

Phone: 868-5300

Price: $10 and under per person

Hours: Sunday - Wednesday 11 a.m. - 11 p.m.

Thursday - Saturday 11 a.m. - 2 a.m.

### JP's Eatery

Food: Pizza, subs

Address: 38 Main St.

Durham, N.H.

Phone: 868-7449

Price: $10 and under per person

Hours: Monday - Saturday 11 a.m. - 11 p.m.

Sunday 11 a.m. - 9 p.m.

### Mike Libby's Bar & Grill

Food: American

Address: 47 Main St.

Durham, NH

Phone: 868-5542

Price: $10 and under per person

Hours: Lunch/Dinner 11:30 a.m. - 10 p.m.

Bar open until 2 a.m.

### Pauly's Pockets

Food: Subs and sandwiches

Address: Mill Road Plaza

Durham, NH

Phone: 868-3110

Price: $10 and under per person

Hours: Monday - Sunday 11 a.m. - 10 p.m.

### Stat's Place

Food: Subs and sandwiches

Address: 11 Madbury Rd.

Durham, NH

Phone: 868-1146

Price: $10 and under per person

Hours: Sunday - Saturday 11 a.m. - 11 p.m.

### Tin Palace

Food: Subs and sandwiches

Address: 4 Ballard St.

Durham, NH

Phone: 868-7456

Price: $10 and under per person

Hours: Lunch/Dinner 11:30
a.m. - 10 p.m.
Bar open until 2 a.m.

**UNH Dairy Bar**
Food: American
Address: 3 Depot Rd.
Durham, NH
Phone: 868-1006
Cool feature: Amtrak Railroad
Station
Price: $10 and under per
person
Hours: 9 a.m. - 5 p.m.

**Wildcat Pizza**
Food: American
Address: 3 Madbury Rd.
Durham, NH
Phone: 868-5530
Price: $10 and under per
person
Hours: Monday - Sunday 11:30
a.m. - 9 p.m.

**Young's Restaurant & Coffee
Shop**
Food: American/Breakfast
Address: 48 Main St.
Durham, NH
Phone: 868-2688
Price: $10 and under per
person
Hours: 7 a.m. - 2 p.m.

## Student Favorites:
Durham House of Pizza
Libby's Bar and Grill
Murphy's Tin Palace

## Late-Night Dining:
Gumby's: Pokey Stix are two
for one on Tuesdays
Okoboji Grill: Pasta entrees
are two for one on Tuesdays

## Closest Grocery Stores:
Durham Market Place
Mill Road Plaza
Durham, NH
868-2500

## Best Pizza:
Joe's New York Style Pizza

## Best Chinese:
China Buffet

## Best Breakfast:
The Bagelry

## Best Wings:
Tin Palace

## Best Healthy:
Pauly's Pockets

## Best Place to Take Your Parents:
Libby's Bar and Grill

## Late-Night, Half-Price Food Specials:
$1 pizza at Durham House of
Pizza after 11 p.m.

## Students Speak Out On...
# Off-Campus Dining

**"There aren't too many great restaurants off-campus, but two that come to mind are the Portsmouth Brewery and the Muddy River Smoke House."**

Q "The restaurants off-campus are decent. There are a few places downtown where everybody likes to eat. **Most of the restaurants there are take-out type places**. One hot spot is the Durham House of Pizza, which serves dollar slices after eleven o' clock every night. You are always sure to run into someone you know at DHOP."

Q "Pauly's is my favorite place to eat. They have **great fast food, freshly prepared,** and a nice location on Main Street."

Q "Durham is very small. There are a couple of places to eat downtown, such as Durham House of Pizza, Wildcat Pizza, and JP's Eatery. There are a couple bars downtown, including Libby's, The Tap Room, and some others. **Newingtown, about a fifteen-minute car ride away, has more places to eat** and a mall."

Q "Just off-campus, there are many **coffee shops and pizza places worthy of going to.** I recommend Joe's NY style Pizza."

Q "Joe's Pizza is the hot spot on the weekends because they are **good, cheap and open until 4 a.m.!** Also there is JP's Eatery for subs, Acorn's restaurant for fancy dinning and Benjamin's for a good regular restaurant."

Q "If you take a ten minute drive, there are the typical casual restaurants like Applebees, TGI Fridays, and The Olive Garden. Right in town, walking distance from campus, is **Benjamin's, which serves everything,** and is really good."

Q "Durham is pretty small so there aren't many places to eat there, but the take-out food is great up here. **Durham doesn't have many great restaurants**-mostly little places for pizza or subs. There are some actual restaurants, don't get me wrong, but the towns nearby are better."

Q "Downtown Durham has some cool places. JP's is a very good eatery, and **Joe's Pizza is great when you're hungry at 1 a.m.**"

Q "As far as off-campus restaurants, there is a variety of food in Durham, including the best pizza in the world, grinders or subs, cheap Italian, fine Italian, bagels, coffee, and ice cream. For more variety, Portsmouth is a short car or bus ride away and has **some of the best food in New England,** located right on Portsmouth's coastal harbor"

Q "Off-campus, there are many restaurants. If you drive about fifteen minutes, there's an **Olive Garden, Friday's, Applebee's, and a few others**"

# The College Prowler Take On...
# Off-Campus Dining

The town of Durham is small, and unfortunately, so is the selection of restaurants. Most students don't have the time or money to go to the better places further off campus. So, most of the time, you will see students hanging out at the local bars and sub shops during the day. At night, the pizza shops, particularly the Durham House of Pizza, are overwhelmed with people grabbing $1 slices at 1 a.m. The Portsmouth Brewery and The Muddy River Smokehouse are two local restaurants that aren't too hard on the wallet and are a part of local tradition.

If you do get an appetite for something more, the shuttle buses run out to Dover, Newmarket, and Portsmouth where you can go to some of the more popular chain restaurants such as Applebees, TGI Friday's, and The Olive Garden. There are plenty of fancy restaurants in Portsmouth that are worth visiting as well; it's just a matter of getting a bunch of friends together and spending a night out on the town.

**B-**

The College Prowler™ Grade on

## Off-Campus Dining: B-

A high off-campus dining grade implies that off-campus restaurants are affordable, accessible, and worth visiting. Other factors include the variety of cuisine and the availability of alternative options (vegetarian, vegan, Kosher, etc.).

# Campus Housing

**The Lowdown On...**
## Campus Housing

## Room Types:

**Singles:** Found in the dorms and are rather small depending on which dorm. Come with bed desk chair and closet
Doubles: Most common in dorms and have everything for two people

**Triples:** Also a common room in freshman dorms.
Forced Triple: Double rooms fit for three people. This is due to a shortage of space in dorms, but they are broken up with in the first few months of school as new spots open up.

**Quads:** Four person rooms which are usually study lounges turned into dorm rooms.

**Suites:** Mills Hall is the only suite dorm. These rooms can hold five to eight students. The rooms have common living areas with furniture and a private bathroom with showers.

**Apartments:** There are two on-campus apartment complexes (Woodsides and Gables). They range from four to six person apartments and include a full size living room, dining table and kitchen area

➡

# Number of Dorms:

20

## Best Dorms:
The Upper Quad

Mills Hall

Congreve Hall

## Worst Dorms:
Stoke

Williamson

Christiansen

## Dormitories:

### Stoke Hall
Floors: 8
Total Occupancy: 600+
Bathrooms: two per floor
Co-Ed: Yes
Percentage of Men/Women:
50/50
Percentage of First-Year Students: 85%
Room Types: Singles, doubles,
triples and quads
Special Features: laundry
room, game room, Snack bar

### Congreve Hall
Floors: 4
Total Occupancy: 276
Bathrooms: per floor
Co-Ed: Yes
Percentage of Men/Women:
40/60
Percentage of First-Year Students: 56%
Room Types: Singles, doubles,
triples and quads
Special Features: Kitchen,
fireplace, piano, TV recreation
lounge

### Jessie Doe Hall
Floors: 4
Total Occupancy: 140
Bathrooms: per floor
Co-Ed: Yes
Percentage of Men/Women:
50/50
Percentage of First-Year Students: 61%
Room Types: Singles, doubles
and Triples, Quads.
Special Features: kitchen, fireplace, patio, piano

### Lord Hall
Floors: 4
Total Occupancy: 120
Bathrooms: per floor
Co-Ed: Yes
Percentage of Men/Women:
50/50
Percentage of First-Year Students: 75%
Room Types: Singles, doubles,
triples and quads.
Special Features: fireplace,
kitchen and ping pong table

### McLaughlin Hall
Floors: 3
Total Occupancy: 127
Bathrooms: per floor
Co-Ed: Yes
Percentage of Men/Women:
40/60
Percentage of First-Year Students: 60%
Room Types: Singles, doubles,
triples and quads
Special Features: game room,
kitchen, fireplace, next to Whittemore Center

### Sawyer Hall
Floors: 4
Total Occupancy: 142
Bathrooms: per floor
Co-Ed: Yes
Percentage of Men/Women: 50/50
Percentage of First-Year Students: 60%
Room Types: Singles, doubles, triples and quads
Special Features: fireplace, TV and study lounge

### Scott Hall
Floors: 4
Total Occupancy: 117
Bathrooms: per floor
Co-Ed: no
Percentage of Men/Women: 0/100
Percentage of First-Year Students: 60%
Room Types: Singles, doubles, triples and quads
Special Features: fireplace, kitchen, piano, front porch and handicap accessible

### Smith Hall
Floors: 5
Total Occupancy: 91
Bathrooms: per floor
Co-Ed: Yes
Percentage of Men/Women: 45/55
Percentage of First-Year Students: 63%
Room Types: Singles, doubles, triples and quads
Special Features: kitchen, fireplace, great porch, handicap accessible

### Alexander Hall
Floors: 3
Total Occupancy: 148
Bathrooms: per floor
Co-Ed: Yes
Percentage of Men/Women: 45/55
Percentage of First-Year Students: 100%
Room Types: Singles, doubles, triples and quads
Special Features: fireplace, piano and foosball

### Devine Hall
Floors: 5
Total Occupancy: 300
Bathrooms: per floor
Co-Ed: Yes
Percentage of Men/Women: 30/70
Percentage of First-Year Students: 45%
Room Types: Singles, doubles, triples and quads
Special Features: Fireplace, kitchen, private courtyard, community desk, ping pong table

### Hitchcock Hall
Floors: 4
Total Occupancy: 250
Bathrooms: per floor
Co-Ed: Yes
Percentage of Men/Women: 40/60
Percentage of First-Year Students: 40%
Room Types: Singles, doubles, triples and quads
Special Features: Fireplace, kitchen, private courtyard, community desk, ping pong table

➜

## Randall Hall
Floors: 5
Total Occupancy: 210
Bathrooms: per floor
Co-Ed: Yes
Percentage of Men/Women: 50/50
Percentage of First-Year Students: 45%
Room Types: Singles, doubles, triples and quads
Special Features: Fireplace, kitchen, private courtyard, community desk, ping pong table

## Engelhardt Hall
Floors: 3
Total Occupancy: 122
Bathrooms: per floor
Co-Ed: Yes
Percentage of Men/Women: 55/45
Percentage of First-Year Students: 55%
Room Types: Singles, doubles, triples and quads
Special Features: Lounge, Bike storage, foosball

## Gibbs Hall
Floors: 3
Total Occupancy: 127
Bathrooms: per floor
Co-Ed: Yes
Percentage of Men/Women: 50/50
Percentage of First-Year Students: 60%
Room Types: Singles, doubles, triples and quads
Special Features: Lounge, courtyard, volleyball and basketball courts in backyard

## Fairchild Hall
Floors: 4
Total Occupancy: 156
Bathrooms: per floor
Co-Ed: Yes
Percentage of Men/Women: 40/60
Percentage of First-Year Students: 50%
Room Types: Singles, doubles, triples and quads
Special Features: kitchen, lounge, piano

## Hetzel Hall
Floors: 4
Total Occupancy: 164
Bathrooms: per floor
Co-Ed: Yes
Percentage of Men/Women: 40/60
Percentage of First-Year Students: 40%
Room Types: Singles, doubles, triples and quads
Special Features: Main street location, piano, ping pong, lounges

## Hunter Hall
Floors: 3
Total Occupancy: 125
Bathrooms: per floor
Co-Ed: Yes
Percentage of Men/Women: 50/50
Percentage of First-Year Students: 50%
Room Types: Singles, doubles, triples and quads
Special Features: Handicap accessible, lower quad courtyard

## Christensen Hall
Floors: 10
Total Occupancy: 440
Bathrooms: per floor
Co-Ed: YeS

## Eaton House

Floors: 2
Total Occupancy: 50
Bathrooms: per floor
Co-Ed: Yes
Percentage of Men/Women: 50/50
Percentage of First-Year Students: 50%
Room Types: Singles, doubles, triples and quads
Special Features: piano, kitchen, lounge, sundeck

## Marston House

Floors: 2
Total Occupancy: 50
Bathrooms: per floor
Co-Ed: Yes
Percentage of Men/Women: 50/50
Percentage of First-Year Students: 50%
Room Types: Singles, doubles, triples and quads
Special Features: piano, kitchen, lounge, sundeck

## Richardson House

Floors: 2
Total Occupancy: 50
Bathrooms: per floor
Co-Ed: Yes
Percentage of Men/Women: 50/50
Percentage of First-Year Students: 50%
Room Types: Singles, doubles, triples and quads
Special Features: piano, kitchen, lounge, sundeck

## Hall House

Floors: 2
Total Occupancy: 50
Bathrooms: per floor
Co-Ed: Yes
Percentage of Men/Women: 50/50
Percentage of First-Year Students: 50%
Room Types: Singles, doubles, triples and quads
Special Features: piano, kitchen, lounge, sundeck, rock climbing wall

## Sackett House

Floors: 2
Total Occupancy: 50
Bathrooms: per floor
Co-Ed: Yes
Percentage of Men/Women: 50/50
Percentage of First-Year Students: 50%
Room Types: Singles, doubles, triples and quads
Special Features: piano, kitchen, lounge, sundeck

## Woodruff House

Floors: 2
Total Occupancy: 50
Bathrooms: per floor
Co-Ed: Yes
Percentage of Men/Women: 50/50
Percentage of First-Year Students: 50%
Room Types: Singles, doubles, triples and quads
Special Features: piano, kitchen, lounge, sundeck

**Hubbard Hall**
Floors: 4
Total Occupancy: 210
Bathrooms: per floor
Co-Ed: Yes
Percentage of Men/Women:
50/50
Percentage of First-Year Students: 65%
Room Types: Singles, doubles, triples and quads
Special Features: piano, kitchen, lounge, area 3 entertainment center, volleyball court

**Williamson Hall**
Floors: 10
Total Occupancy: 440
Bathrooms: per floor
Co-Ed: Yes
Percentage of Men/Women:
50/50
Percentage of First-Year Students: 100%
Room Types: Singles, doubles, triples and quads
Special Features: kitchen, lounge, sundeck, basketball court, volleyball court

## Undergrads on Campus: 50%

**Students living in Singles:** 19%

**Students living in Doubles:** 58%

**Students living in Triples/Suites:** 6%

**Students living in Apartments:** 17%

## Bed Type
Single in all University-Owned rooms

## Cleaning Service?
In all dorms and campus apartments only, a few times a week.

## What You Get
Bed, desk and chair, bookshelf, dresser, closet or wardrobe, window coverings, cable TV jack, Ethernet or broadband internet connections, free campus and local phone calls

## Also Available:
Themed Housing: There are different themes for certain dorms such as, Chem-Free, The Clubhouse, Multicultural Living, Community Service, Whittemore School of Business, First Year Student Experience, Honors Program, International Living, Living in Harmony, Academic, Outdoor Experiential Education, Performing Arts, Science and Engineering, Tomorrows Educators, Visual Arts, Wired, and All Female.

> **"The dorms are good. For freshmen, I recommend Hubbard, Sawyer, or Alexander. Mills is the nicest upperclassmen dorm."**

Q "The dorm you choose depends on what you want out of school. If you want to be able to walk out your door and onto frat row, you should stay in the biggest dorm, Stoke. Williamson and Christiansen are far away from the parties but close to the school. The Gables is in the middle of nowhere but there are no RAs, so **you can have parties and stuff without anyone watching you.**"

Q "The dorms are all right; they're nothing spectacular, but a **great place to meet people.**"

Q "All the **dorms are nice.** Anything in area one is really good."

Q "Some dorms are nice, and some dorms are not so nice. As freshmen, you may choose to live in an all-freshman dorm or somewhere else. **Your typical room has two people, two beds, desks,** etc. It's hard getting used to living in such a small space with another person, but dorm life is really great (you get to know so many new people). As upperclassmen, it becomes easier to get into nicer dorms, such as the suite-style dorms or the on-campus apartments, but this is not possible for freshmen."

Q "The dorms are pretty nice for the most part. Avoid the freshmen dorms and Stoke Hall if at all possible. Mills and Congreve are the nicest dorms. **Mills has suite style housing** and Congreve holds mostly singles."

Q "I think all the dorms are really nice and **I don't see any that need to be avoided**. Some are newer than others though, such as Congreve or Mills."

Q "If you can get into Congreve or Mills, go for it. They're brand new. I would stay away from the freshmen dorms like Christianson, Williamson, and Stoke. **They are huge, crowded, and usually dirty.** The dorms in the upper quad are nice, and the rooms are a good size. Englehart is the chem-free dorm, and there are many other themed dorms to pick from."

Q "Live in Christensen or Williamson as a freshman! All of the freshmen **dorms are so much fun and everyone is so friendly**-I miss it a lot."

Q "Some of the dorms are better than others. I would avoid Stoke Hall. Hubbard Hall is very nice because the rooms are bigger than most, and **Congreve Hall has a very good location."**

Q "Overall, the dorms are a **good size and there aren't too many problems**. Freshmen dorms are kind of far from classes, but they are nice because all the residents are freshmen. You'll have some of the best times of your life here."

Q "The dorms at UNH are great. There **seems to be one for everyone**, so there aren't any to avoid. There are dorms near downtown, larger ones, smaller ones, ones near classes, secluded ones, ones near the gym or food courts, and even ones that have themes to go along with what you're into."

Q "Most of the dorms are pretty nice. I've seen better at other schools, but they're not bad at UNH. Definitely live in freshmen dorms for freshman year. They're not as nice as some of the others, but you'll want the experience to **be with other people who are going through the same things you are."**

## The College Prowler Take On...
# Campus Housing

UNH has a dorm to suit anyone's style. Whether you're a double major in Biology and Mathematics who wants nothing more then a quiet living space to study and be in close proximity to the Science and Math buildings, or a party animal jock whose soul purpose in life is to be the center of attention, there is probably a dorm for you. There are large freshmen dorms that aren't as pretty as other dorms (Christianson, Williamson, Stoke), but the people you meet there and relationships you form are hard to come by anywhere other than on campus. Some disadvantages to freshmen dorms are the loud atmospheres, dirty hallways and bathrooms, and the sometimes long walks to classes. Themed halls (Smith, The Clubhouse) are also a big part of helping students find others that have similar interests. There are many themes including Chemical Free Dorms, Multicultural dorms, Business Dorms, and even all female dorms (males need not apply).

Most students agree that your chances of getting into a dorm other than a freshmen dorm are slim, due to increasing freshman class sizes, but it's worth the effort to try. Living with people other than freshmen can have great advantages. Upperclassmen have a better sense of the school and experience that most freshmen will not be able to provide. The biggest advantage is the newer and nicer rooms you will enjoy. Whatever your style is you can find a place to fit in at UNH.

### The College Prowler™ Grade on
### Campus Housing: B+

A high Campus Housing grade indicates that dorms are clean, well-maintained, and spacious. Other determining factors include variety of dorms, proximity to classes, and social atmosphere.

# Off-Campus Housing

The Lowdown On...
## Off-Campus Housing

**Undergrads in
Off-Campus Housing:**
60%

**Average Rent for a
Studio Apartment:**
$150-$200/month

**Average Rent for a
1BR Apartment:**
$300-$350/month

**Average Rent for a
2BR Apartment:**
$400 - $500/month

**Best Time to Look
for a Place:**
At the start of the second semester for the next year.

**Popular Areas:**
Main street in Durham
Dover
Newmarket

## Students Speak Out On...
# Off-Campus Housing

> **"Off-campus housing is difficult to get and costs as much as it does to live on campus, but it is close to campus and offers more freedom."**

Q "Living off-campus is definitely worth it. **Newmarket and Dover are great places** and the bus system makes it all that much easier."

Q "There is a lot of off-campus housing, but it goes quickly and is **very expensive in Durham.** Many students live in the dorms until junior year, and if they do not move into the on-campus apartments, Gables or Woodsides, they try to live outside of Durham in Dover, Lee, or Newmarket because it is cheaper."

Q "Off-campus housing is definitely worth it, and **definitely convenient."**

Q "A lot of people like off-campus housing because you don't have to deal with as much authority and there are a lot of really nice apartments out there. There is housing available in surrounding communities, such as Dover and Newmarket, as well as in Durham.  However, living off campus makes everything a lot less convenient.  When you are living on campus, **everything is right here at your fingertips."**

Q "Off-campus housing is **hard to find freshman year,** and probably not worth it.  You meet a lot of friends living in the dorms."

Q **"Off-campus housing is very convenient,** but I liked living in the residence hall enough that I wanted to stay."

Q "Some people like the **freedoms of living off-campus** and it often costs less. Most people move to Dover or Newmarket."

Q "If you can get an apartment right in downtown, it's nice, but it's very expensive. I would stay on campus through my sophomore year though. They offer on-campus apartments for students, too. If you have a car and don't mind a drive, getting an apartment in Dover might not be a bad idea, although it is **more detached from the whole 'college' feeling.**"

Q "Off-campus housing is pretty convenient; it just **takes a while to find something good.**"

Q "To get a good apartment you need to **start looking early,** but you can find some good ones."

Q "It seems people are always looking for roommates off campus. I think it's kind of hard to get an apartment in Durham, but many students get apartments in Dover and Newmarket, the two surrounding towns. There are **plenty of options for an apartment.**"

Q "The **quality of off-campus housing depends on many circumstances**, but overall, it's convenient."

# The College Prowler Take On...
# Off-Campus Housing

UNH is surrounded by small rural towns, with the exception of Portsmouth. Most students who choose to live off-campus move to the neighboring towns of Dover and Newmarket. Rent prices in the two towns are very reasonable. A house for five people could range anywhere from $1000 to $2000 depending on certain amenities. Through the UNH website, students can search for off-campus housing relatively easy. Most renters in these towns welcome students. Shuttles frequently run out to these two towns and make for an easy ten or twenty-minute commute to campus. Both Dover and Newmarket are similar in atmosphere, both being very casual small towns. Portsmouth is a little less convenient. It is the closest city to Durham and has just what you would expect from a city, high rent prices and mostly small apartments. Consequently, the student population is quite small in Portsmouth. A university shuttle does run out to Portsmouth, making life there entirely possible, if you don't mind the city and the higher prices.

Living in Durham itself is a much sought after treasure, for its most obvious reason of being able to walk to school and being close to the atmosphere of UNH. Finding a place to live in Durham is not easy, but also not impossible. The rent tends to be slightly higher than Dover or Newmarket, but bargains do surface here and there. Off-campus housing at UNH is very abundant and provides you with many choices to choose a place that you genuinely like.

The College Prowler™ Grade on

## Off-Campus Housing: C+

A high grade in Off-Campus Housing indicates that apartments are of high quality, close to campus, affordable, and easy to secure.

# Diversity

The Lowdown On...
## Diversity

**American Indian:**
0%

**Asian or Pacific Islander:**
2%

**African American:**
1%

**Hispanic:**
1%

**White:**
96%

**International:**
1%

**Out-of-State:**
41%

## Political Activity:

UNH tends to be very politically active, especially around the Presidential Primaries.

## Gay Tolerance:

UNH is very accepting of the gay culture, and they are very prominent on-campus holding many events tailored specifically to the gay community as well as gay awareness.

## Most Popular Religions:

UNH has a very active Christian Fellowship and Jewish organization, and new groups are popping up every year.

## Economic Status:

The economic status tends to lean more toward the upper-class, with many students from rich prominent towns in southern New Hampshire and Massachusetts. However, UNH is a state school, and there are many "blue collar" students as well.

## Minority Clubs:

The Office of Multicultural Students Association (OMSA) is a very hardworking student organization. They hold numerous events to help raise awareness of student minorities and to give minorities and great way to meet people.

## Students Speak Out On...
# Diversity

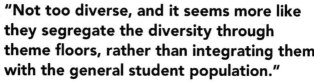

"Not too diverse, and it seems more like they segregate the diversity through theme floors, rather than integrating them with the general student population."

Q "The campus isn't very diverse, but it **does not seem to be an issue.**"

Q "UNH is about **99.999 percent white.**"

Q "Different races are present. There's an international dorm and a Spanish-speaking one. The people you meet are so different from high school people. **Everyone is family, and no one is judged.** There are gays, different religions, different majors, and so on. You'll meet so many totally different, really cool people."

Q "I won't lie; UNH is **not a poster school for diversity.**"

Q "UNH is fairly diverse, but it generally **reflects the state of New Hampshire itself.**"

Q "The campus isn't that diverse by the statistics they give students, but then again, **I have met a diverse group of people.** I had one girl on my floor from Japan, and I also have many African-American friends from the football team."

Q "I **don't see a very diverse campus** here. Most of the students are white."

Q "The school is not very diverse at all. I think **races other than white make up about four percent** of the population."

Q "Diversity is a work in progress for UNH. They are trying to implement new programs to increase diversity on campus. It's not great right now, but it is present. There are **plenty of clubs that encourage diversity**, so it's there if you want it."

Q "It's a **lot of white kids running around** here!"

Q "This is a hard question to answer because there are a lot of different people. New England, in general, is not known for its diversity, and I suppose there's an **overall preppy theme on campus**, but there are always people who are different."

# The College Prowler Take On...
# Diversity

UNH administration has long been assigned the difficult task of trying to bring diversity to a small campus in the middle of New England. Generally, New Hampshire is not a state that appeals to diverse students. This may never change. Many minority students will have to travel great distances to come here and will, consequently, be far from their own cultures. On the other hand, most of the multicultural students here are actually long time New Hampshire residents.

For minority students who do come to UNH, the campus tries very hard to make the transition an easy one. There are many student run organizations, such as OMSA, that help students keep in touch with their culture and meet new people with similar cultures. The Multicultural themed dorm is one option, but some students feel that these dorms have a tendency to separate minority students rather than integrate them into the general student population. While it's true that UNH may never become a poster school for diversity, students and student administration should continue the attempt to diversify the campus by all means.

D-

The College Prowler™ Grade on
## Diversity: D-

A high grade in Diversity indicates that ethnic minorities and international students have a notable presence on campus and that students of different economic backgrounds, religious beliefs, and sexual preferences are well-represented.

# Guys & Girls

The Lowdown On...
## Guys & Girls

**Men Undergrads:**
43%

**Women Undergrads:**
57%

**Birth Control Available?**
Yes, in the Health Services Department

**Most Prevalent STDs on Campus:**
Genital Warts

**Percentage of Students with an STD:**
5%

## Social Scene:

Every student at UNH desires to make the most out of their college experiences. Almost everyone is friendly to some extent. Every weekend there is a party to be found or an event where people can meet others, but mostly the only places people meet on the weekends are the fraternity parties. Outside of parties, classes and the library are the next best thing. Study partners are a great way to meet prospective lovers or just good friends.

## Hookups or Relationships?

With the large Greek party presence on the weekends, the bulk of student relationships are formed in random hookups, but relationships seem to be found everywhere where students meet and interact. Most random hookups from frat parties tend to evolve into relationships as well (some more serious than others).

## Best Place to Meet Guys/Girls:

Obviously the frat parties are the number one place to meet people looking to have a good time, since the majority of people at the parties are people you do not know. Other than that, the next best thing is to hang out downtown at the bar or the local pizza shops where lots of people flock early in the morning.

## Did You Know?

**Top Three Places to Find Hotties:**

Frat parties

The dining halls

Scorpions Bar

**Top Places to Hookup:**

In your single dorm room.

In the dorm shower.

A random room at an apartment party.

Dorm lounge.

In the bushes on the walk home.

## Dress Code:

The Greek look can range from hipster casual with the fake authentic trucker hat to a Polo shirt with the stonewashed jeans. Pink seems to be coming back as a guy color. The next biggest fashion trend is complete abandonment of trends. In other words, the less you seem to care about appearance (to a certain extent of course) the more desired you'll be to the opposite sex. The dirtier your hair is, the more original you'll seem. It's beginning to be all about originality at UNH. Birkenstocks, in some cases, are a must. Due to the colder climates the closed-toed Birks are the best. Another popular trend is the classical grunge skater garb. When it comes to fashion, basically anything goes at UNH.

Duxbury Free Library

## Students Speak Out On...
# Guys & Girls

"Whatever your type, you'll find them at UNH. Both the guys and the girls are attractive There are eighteen to twenty-three year-olds everywhere, so of course you'll be drooling-I know I was!"

Q "There are **a lot of gorgeous women** everywhere!"

Q "The guys can be rather, well, thick-headed here, and some of the girls are rather ditzy. But I have found **lots of very intelligent, cool people.** And yes, there are lots of hot women here."

Q "The **girls at UNH are very hot.**"

Q **"There are a lot of hot mountain men,** but a lot of the guys/girls look the same."

Q "The **guys and girls are both really nice.** If you need help with something, I wouldn't feel bad walking up to a stranger to ask a question. I think that most of the guys on campus are okay looking, some are better than others. We have a fair share of hippies, too, and to me they seem dirtier than the rest of the population."

Q "There are cute guys and girls, but unfortunately, **girls outnumber guys three-to-one** or something like that."

Q "There are large variations in the people at UNH. We have a lot of hippies, but also a lot of the preppy, Abercrombie type, and the 'pretty-boy' type. For the most part, the **campus is very much 'all-American'**. I think there are lots of hot guys here, as long as you like all-American boys."

Q "In general, UNH is a very nice-looking campus. The guys are hot, but there are a lot of jerks. There are also a lot of awesome guys too, so it all depends on who you involve yourself with. I think that most girls at UNH are very friendly and chill. I have met some of my best friends here, and I think that it's a **very friendly and accepting campus.**"

Q "Like any place on this planet, there are beautiful people and **people who are beauty-challenged.**"

# The College Prowler Take On...
# Guys & Girls

Ah yes, the ultimate question on any prospective students mind. Are the girls/guys hot? The answer at UNH is "yes" and "no." This is the answer anyone will give because of the wide variety of students attending UNH. Since the school is fairly large, there is every type of beauty imaginable. There are the traditional pretty-boys and sorority girls, as well as the sporty types, the smart types, the girls and guys next door, the dirty hippies, rugged mountain men, and those who might not grace the cover of the next YM magazine. Anyway that you look at it, there is someone for everyone. It's safe to say that, in the looks department, the guys and girls at UNH won't disappoint.

All students agree that no matter what your taste in guys or girls is, everyone is generally friendly and accepting of whatever type of beauty you may possess. As far as meeting people goes, it's all in the effort. Guys at UNH (Especially Freshmen) must realize that they're going to get "shot down" every once in a while, and girls shouldn't fall head over heels in love with every other rugged lumberjack looking fellow either (Don't worry ladies, there are plenty of trees out there that haven't been chopped down yet). Considering the size of UNH, finding companionship of the opposite sex won't be easy but, with the right attitude, at least you'll have fun trying.

**The College Prowler™ Grade on**
Guys: B

A high grade for Guys indicates that the male population on campus is attractive, smart, friendly, and engaging, and that the school has a decent ratio of guys to girls.

**The College Prowler™ Grade on**
Girls: A-

A high grade for Girls not only implies that the women on campus are attractive, smart, friendly, and engaging, but also that there is a fair ratio of girls to guys.

# Athletics

**The Lowdown On...**
## Athletics

**Athletic Division:**
Division I in a majority of sports

**Number of Males in Varsity Sports:**
232 (4%)

**Number of Females in Varsity Sports:**
271 (3%)

**Intercollegiate Varsity Sports:**

**Men's Teams:**
Hockey
Basketball
Soccer
Football
Indoor/Outdoor Track
Skiing
Tennis
Cross Country
Swimming/Diving

→

**Women's Teams:**
Basketball
Crew
Field Hockey
Volleyball
Gymnastics
Ice Hockey
Indoor Track
Lacrosse
Outdoor Track
Skiing
Soccer
Swimming/Diving
Tennis

## Club Sports:
Aikido
Archery
Baseball
Crew - men's
Cycling
Dance
Fencing
Figure Skating
Golf - men's
Golf - Women's
Judo
Lacrosse
Rifle
Rugby - men/women
Sailing
Shotokan karate
Softball
Tae Kwon Do
Volleyball
Wrestling

## Intramurals:
Indoor/Outdoor Soccer
Kickball
Softball
Flag football
Broomball
Volleyball
Off season 5 on 5 basketball
Women's Field Hockey
Ultimate Frisbee
Golf
Billiards
Basketball
Hockey
Floor Hockey
Dodgeball
Table Tennis
Tennis
Racquetteball
4-on-4 Flag football
Track and Field

## Most Popular Sports:
Hockey
Soccer
Football
Women's Lacross
Field Hockey
Ultimate Frisbee

## Overlooked Teams:
Tennis
Skiing
Volleyball
Swimming

## Fields/Facilities

Memorial Field (short turf), Upper Field (long turf), Boulder Field, Track and Field, Football, Soccer, Rugby, Baseball

**The Whittemore Center:** This arena holds the ice rink and is a privately owned building that UNH rents for games and concerts.

**Hamel Recreation Center:** This building is the student exercise center. It has two floor rinks, 5 basketball courts, 4 racquetteball courts, three exercise studios, a weight room and bathroom facilities with saunas and showers.

**The Field House:** This area is used for the athletics department and has an indoor pool for public use during certain times. There is also the basketball court for the men and women's basketball teams and the volleyball teams. There is a gymnastics training center as well as performance training center. There is also an indoor track.

## School Mascot

Wild E. Cat

## Getting Tickets

Tickets to almost all sports are free to students and very easy to get even for the men's hockey games.

## Best Place to Take a Walk

College woods and the walkways around campus in the spring

## Students Speak Out On...
# Athletics

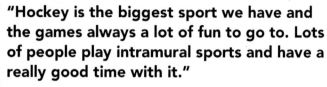

**"Hockey is the biggest sport we have and the games always a lot of fun to go to. Lots of people play intramural sports and have a really good time with it."**

Q "Both varsity and intramural **sports are very big at UNH."**

Q "Intramural sports are big on campus. A lot of times people will play on an intramural team with their floor or residence hall. As far as varsity sports, UNH students take a lot of pride in the hockey team. **Games always sell out.**"

Q "The hockey team is the major attraction here at UNH, and it is a lot of fun to go watch the games in the Whitt. **There are lots of IM sports,** like soccer and broomball."

Q "Both Intramural sports and varsity athletics are huge. Many **students (eighty percent) at UNH participate in athletics** at some level."

Q "Varsity sports are pretty big. Ice hockey is huge for girls and guys. Football is doing well, and so are men's and women's basketball. I play basketball, and we had huge crowds this year. The sports community is awesome. **We all support each other**-it's great. Volleyball is big, too."

Q **"Hockey is the only sport I ever hear a fuss about."**

Q "Hockey is huge! It's so much fun. Intramurals are big too-especially **broomball. It's a college-created sport."**

Q "Intramural sports are very popular at UNH. **Many dorms start their own leagues** for a variety of sports. One of the most popular intramural sports is 'broomball', which is played on the ice hockey rink. Varsity sports are big when the team is good. Our hockey team has been really good and has gone far in the past. Hockey games are always fun to go to. Football is pretty popular, as well as Rugby and Soccer."

Q "UNH is huge in sports. They are so much fun to root for, especially our **nationally ranked hockey team.** Even if you're not into sports, you'll enjoy all the good-looking athletes."

Q "Hockey is huge! Everyone loves the hockey team because they are really good! **It's free for students to go to any game they want,** so be sure to go. It is really fun! IM is pretty big. I'm not really athletic, but I played IM basketball and football. Just get involved if you live in the dorm-ask your hall council or your HD about IM sports. Almost every dorm has a team for every sport."

Q "I would say, besides men's hockey, **the second most popular sport is Ultimate Frisbee.** There are always people playing it somewhere on campus."

Q "Both varsity and intramurals are huge! Our hockey team is incredible, so basically the whole school goes to watch them play. **Intramurals are always going on,** from volleyball to floor hockey to soccer. There is always an intramural team to play on. If you are an athlete, I would suggest doing both. I played a few intramurals and it was so fun. I was also a member of the cheerleading team, and that was the greatest time ever."

# The College Prowler Take On...
# Athletics

If you like hockey, UNH is most definitely your place. UNH is home to the Wildcats who have been a perennial powerhouse in Division I hockey for a long time. Unfortunately, hockey tends to overshadow many other varsity sports that the university has to offer. UNH is competitive in football, soccer, track and field, volleyball, basketball, alpine skiing, and also boasts one of the best intramural programs in New England. Hockey draws the most students to its games, but ultimately, no matter which sport you choose to play you will always have students cheering you on.

Intramural sports are a big deal to the students of UNH. While those who win don't get any endorsements or signing bonuses, they do get a t-shirt and just about all the respect you could ever need. Many dorms, fraternities, sororities, student organizations and good friends go for the glory each year. The department of residential life hosts a contest between all the dorms on the campus called the Cat Cup. The basic premise is to see who can do the best in the most intramural sports. Points are awarded for the number of intra-mural sports you play and more points are awarded if you do well in those sports. Programs like this seem to boost student participation tremendously. Although varsity athletes are not allowed to participate, the competition tends to be very fierce. Overall, the students at UNH aren't about big national titles, but the students getting their chance to show off some skills. Although, the students still save time to cheer the Wild-cats hockey team to the national championship each year.

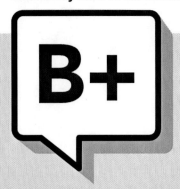

**B+**

The College Prowler™ Grade on

Athletics: B+

A high grade in Athletics indicates that students have school spirit, that sports programs are respected, that games are well-attended, and that intramurals are a prominent part of student life.

# Nightlife

**The Lowdown On...**
## Nightlife

### Club and Bar Prowler: Popular Nightlife Spots!

#### Club Crawler:

Unfortunately there aren't any clubs close by, only in Boston.

#### Bar Prowler:

**Tin Palace**
Address:  4 Ballard St.
Durham, NH
Phone: 868-7456

### Other Places to Check Out:

Murphy's Tin Palace is the only bar with live music every Thursday night.

They have a nice patio with tables and chairs that many students call home during the warm days and nights.

→

### Libby's Bar and Grill

Address: 47 Main St.
Durham, NH
Phone: 868-5542

Libby's Bar and Grill is the nicest of the bars on-campus. During the day it has a family restaurant feel to it, and at night the more tame students enjoy the company of others or enjoy the music and a pool table. Recently, Libby's has started a rule that anyone who comes to Libby's planning to celebrate their twenty-first birthday will be given a free shot and a meal voucher then will be asked to leave. This is due to numerous problems that have occurred in the past.

## Favorite Drinking Games:

Beer Pong
Card Games
Century Club
Quarters
Power Hour

## Local Specialties:

The Scorpion Bowl (Scorpions Bar): No one is sure quite what is in it, but there is definitely a lot of it.

## Cheapest Place to Get a Drink:

Murphy's Tin Palace - Thursday nights $1 pitcher of beer

## Student Favorites:

Libby's
Tin Palace
Breaking New Grounds
DHOP
Joe's Pizza

## Useful Resources for Nightlife:

www.unh.edu
www.ci.durham.nh.us

## Bars Close At:

2 a.m.

## Primary Areas with Nightlife:

Durham Mainstreet
Portsmouth

# What to Do if You're Not 21:

## Breaking New Grounds

Address: 50B Main St.

Durham, NH

Phone: 868-6869

BNG is a favorite of the intellectuals and those not old enough to hit the bars. The Coffee is always good, the music is always refreshing and it is open until 11:30 p.m. most nights. BNG has its own patio furniture and is also a great place to relax on a warm night.

# Organization Parties:

As far as organized parties go, the town of Durham isn't really a partying town. So, other than private parties on campus, there isn't much else going on.

# Frats

See the Greek Section!

## Students Speak Out On...
# Nightlife

"There are two clubs that are close by, but they are kind of sketchy. There are a few bars on campus, but Boston is only an hour away and there are so many bars and clubs there."

Q "There are **a lot of other activities to do if you are not into partying** and drinking, so don't worry."

Q "If you wanted to go off-campus, **Portsmouth is the best place to go**. It has a lot of bars and great night life."

Q "If you wanted to go out off-campus, Portsmouth is the best place to go. They have **a lot of bars and a great nightlife**. There are a few bars on campus, including Libby's, The Tap Room, The Hair of The Dog, and The Tin Palace. I am not twenty-one yet, but from what I have heard from friends and what I've seen, it seems like Libby's is the best place to go on campus, although the food is very good at The Tin Palace and they have a lot of live bands."

Q "On campus the night life **isn't really interesting until Thursday, Friday and Saturday** nights."

Q "The **fraternities tend to dominate the night life at UNH,** but there are always small parties to go to if you know the right people."

Q "Durham **doesn't really offer much to those under twenty-one**, but if you're old enough there are plenty of small local bars that have great late night patrons."

Q "There are a few good bars close to campus. The best one probably would be Murphy's Tin Palace. There are **probably better house parties to go to than a bar** though."

Q "The bars on campus tend to be **pretty strict on fake IDs and underage drinking."**

Q "In my experience, there are two types of parties on campus. The first is the big frat party, which seems to be the scene for a lot of freshman girls. That's cool if you like getting hit on by sketchy guys and leaving with vomit all over your pants. The second type of party on campus is the small apartment party. We have two on-campus apartment complexes that host parties quite often, and they are good for a more intimate party, if you want to meet people and get to know them. Regardless, this is UNH, **there's always something fun going on."**

Q "The parties on campus are **limited because of noise rules, as well as a 'no-keg' rule.** A lot of on-campus apartments also throw 'themed' parties. There are many off-campus apartments that throw good parties, and usually have a friendly atmosphere. Frat Row is usually a happening place to be, but can be crowded and loud. There aren't any clubs downtown, but there are a few bars. Libby's offers a nicer atmosphere. They have a bar upstairs with a huge area to sit and socialize, while downstairs there is a dance floor. Murphy's Tin Palace is not as nice as Libby's but offers a louder, more comfortable atmosphere. The food there is great, too. There is a dance floor downstairs, and they have scheduled bands that come and play."

Q "The **parties on campus are awesome.** I don't know anything about the bars or clubs, but I've heard Libby's and The Tin Palace are good spots."

Q "There **aren't really any clubs in town.** There are a few bars, Libby's and the Tin Palace, etc."

# The College Prowler Take On...
# Nightlife

Unfortunately, if you're not into parties at all, you may be a little hard-pressed to find a lot going on after hours on or around campus. UNH is dominated by the party scene from Thursday to Sunday and sometimes lasts the whole week. Although many parties aren't Greek oriented, Frat Row is the place to go for true authentic college raging! Before or after these parties, many students go to the bars downtown that offer live music, dancing, and alcohol. Apartment parties and off-campus parties are also a big hit with UNH students who enjoy a more intimate setting and more relaxed atmosphere. Just about anybody should be able to find their niche at either of these two types of social events.

For those who are underage, or just uninterested with the party scene, the campus does their best to provide alternative entertainment with events such as concerts, movies, and performances in the MUB. Most weekends, though, the campus is taken over by parties as the main form of enjoyment. Even though there aren't any clubs within the Durham area, the majority of UNH students feel that the nightlife is in no way lacking because of the lack thereof. However, if you come from a big city, such as Boston or New York, the nightlife at and around UNH might not be what you're looking for.

**The College Prowler™ Grade on**
## Nightlife: C

A high grade in Nightlife indicates that there are many bars and clubs in the area that are easily accessible and affordable. Other determining factors include the number of options for the under-21 crowd and the prevalence of house parties.

# Greek Life

**The Lowdown On...**
## Greek Life

**Number of Fraternities:**
12

**Number of Sororities:**
5

**Percent of Undergrad Men in Fraternities:**
5%

**Percent of Undergrad Women in Sororities:**
5%

**Other Greek Organizations**
Greek Council
Greek Peer Advisors
Interfraternity Council
Order of Omega
Panhellenic Council

**"The fraternities get a lot of hassle from the school administration, but they aren't that out of control here."**

Q **"Greek life is what you make of it**, either a part of your life or not."

Q "I am a sorority sister here and the Greek system is the largest student organization, but it doesn't dominate the school by any means. The Greek system works very closely with the school and **I love it! Go Greek!"**

Q "The Greek life does not dominate the social scene, but it is a huge part of UNH because **it's where a lot of kids party.** The frat parties are always filled with kids who aren't Greek, and there are millions of on-campus and off-campus apartments where people party. UNH is the number eleven party school in the nation, number two for binge drinking, and number two for petty drug usage. Partying is huge here, but there are also awesome academic programs. People work hard and party hard here. The frats have a lot to do with that."

Q "Some of the **frats are definitely like 'Animal House',** but they are all different."

Q "There are only a couple frats that provide parties on the weekends, other than that **the Greek system isn't very big."**

Q "You can see the **stereotypical people at frats and sororities,** but most of them are just normal college students."

Q "Once you start to grow up in college, you tend to go to more parties at apartments with your friends. **Frats eventually become old news.**"

Q "I must admit, being in the **Greek system at UNH has a lot of advantages.** Rushing and pledging a sorority is a lot of fun."

Q "Greek life is big on-campus, a lot of people pledge sororities or fraternities. They do have parties and such, but it **doesn't dominate the social scene by any means.**"

Q "It definitely doesn't dominate the social scene. **You don't have to go to frats to have a good time.**"

Q "**UNH is ten to fifteen percent Greek,** I think. Frats are good places to party, but there are definitely tons of alternatives."

Q "I'd say **Greek Life dominates at UNH** alright."

Q "The Greek houses are all in one general area of the campus, on what we call 'Frat Row' and yeah, it does dominate the social scene. There are parties down there almost every night of the weekend. Greek life is very popular on-campus, and **the Greeks get involved a lot to help out.**"

## The College Prowler Take On...
# Greek Life

With all the Greek houses being very close to campus and all in the same general area, it is hard for most students to ignore Greek life on the weekends. Overall, the amount of students in the Greeks system is small. However, there are always parties on the weekends and "Frat Row" is where most student enjoy going. The Greek system at UNH is large enough to satisfy those who really want to become involved without shutting out those who choose not to. Not being Greek won't kill your social life, but pledging can make it a lot easier to meet people and keep up with the party scene.

Although the Greek system may dominate the social scene, there are rarely any problems with authorities, despite a couple violations recently that have suspended a couple of fraternities. Contrary to popular belief, the Greek system at UNH is not just there to party. Many Greek organizations are closely tied in with the school system and also help the community in a number of community service programs. However, many students who join fraternities and sororities say that the Greek system at UNH made their experience twice as good, and the people they meet are friends for life.

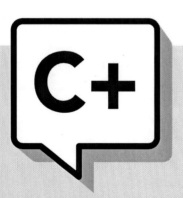

**The College Prowler™ Grade on**
**Greek Life: C+**

A good grade means that Greek life has a highly-visible role on campus. The poorer the grade, the less prominent the Greek scene..

# Drug Scene

The Lowdown On...
## Drug Scene

### Most Prevalent Drugs on Campus:
Marijuana

### Liquor-Related Arrests:
102

### Drug-Related Arrests:
38

### Drug Counseling Programs:
Alcohol and Other Drug (AOD) services are offered by the Office of Health Education and Promotion (OHEP), including the provision of AOD education, assessment, intervention, counseling and referral for UNH students on a voluntary or mandatory basis, as well as training and consultation for UNH staff/faculty.

## Students Speak Out On...
# Drug Scene

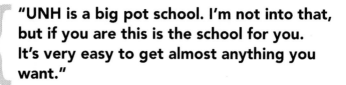

**"UNH is a big pot school. I'm not into that, but if you are this is the school for you. It's very easy to get almost anything you want."**

"It is **as available, or unavailable,** as you want it to be."

"There is a heck of a lot of weed. There are other drugs but, unless you do them, you rarely see them. **Everything is behind closed doors.** There a lot kids that use Ritalin and Adderal to stay awake."

"We have **a lot of potheads.** There are people who do the other stuff, but that's not as common as weed. Most people draw the line at alcohol and marijuana."

"I don't ever see people doing drugs besides weed. I have **heard of people doing Ecstasy and cocaine,** but it was no one I knew or saw. I am not really sure about this because I try to stay away from it."

"There is a heck of a lot of weed. There are other drugs, but unless you do them, you rarely see them. Everything like that is behind closed doors. There are a lot of kids that **use Ritalin and Adderal to stay awake."**

"The drug scene all **depends on the people you surround yourself with** at UNH."

"There is some drug use on campus, but **it is not wide spread."**

Q "There are drugs present at UNH, just as if you went to any other campus. Pot is always big, no matter where you go, but on the other hand, I don't want you to think that we are **a bunch of hippies who just smoke up all day** long. There are probably some that actually will do that, but academically they don't last long. For the most part it's pretty much under control."

Q "I think people **smoke a lot of pot here.**"

Q "I'm not aware of any over-usage of any drug on campus, other than marijuana. I know of a lot of people that smoke. **Alcohol is definitely the number one substance** used on campus."

Q **"Drugs are a big issue with the police,** as is underage drinking and transportation of alcohol. If you drink somewhere private you'll probably be fine. Just carry alcohol in a backpack."

# The College Prowler Take On...
# Drug Scene

Most students see marijuana use happening on a regular basis. Although drug use is basically out in the open, it's rarely a hassle to the students. Some students aren't exposed to any drug use at all. The general consensus is that drugs are basically there if you want them to be.

At UNH, the harder drugs are much less prevalent, and very few cases have been cited. Recently though, a Campus Convenience store was busted for selling weed and some harder drugs over the counter. The store has since been ceased by local authorities. Overall, UNH is a fairly harmless school when it comes to drugs, but ultimately the choice is up to the students.

**C-**

The College Prowler™ Grade on
**Drug Scene: C-**

A good grade means that drugs are not a highly-visible threat on campus. The poorer the grade, the more prominent the drug scene.

# Campus Strictness

**The Lowdown On...**
## Campus Strictness

### What Are You Most Likely to Get Caught Doing on Campus?

- Trying to sneak into bars while underage
- Inciting or participating in a riot
- Getting in a fight at the local bar
- Drinking in public
- Parking in a no-parking spot
- Mouthing off to a police officer
- Smoking weed in college woods or your dorm room

## Students Speak Out On...
# Campus Strictness

> **"There are always campus police driving around at night. They don't usually bother you, though. If you're stumbling and being stupid then they might pull you aside and ask you what's going on, but they're usually harmless."**

Q "The campus police are usually pretty **lenient as long as you are under control."**

Q "If you're not stupid, you will **usually be left alone."**

Q "Campus police suck, but only if you're stupid. If you stumble around outside drunk, they will arrest you if you're underage. If you can be fairly normal when you're drunk, then you're good to go. They do have a tendency to **break up parties if they get too big** and out of control."

Q "The campus administration is getting much stricter on drinking and partying, and also **cracking down on Greek parties."**

Q "The police **don't usually bust parties** until it gets really late, like 3 a.m. or later."

Q "If you're walking with an open container they will stop you, but that's normal. You could **just put anything you want in a backpack."**

Q "UNH is very strict about drinking since **it is a dry campus.** This doesn't mean that UNH students listen to the rules, but you can easily lose housing for getting caught with alcohol or drugs in the dorms. If you have an open beer can outside, you will be arrested on the spot. It's pretty strict but people still seem to get away with it, anyway."

Q "That's another bad thing about this school; **the cops are everywhere on Friday and Saturday** nights."

Q "Since UNH has been put in the spotlight for numerous riots, the campus **police have become very strict.**"

Q "Supposedly, this is a dry campus. Police are out every night patrolling the streets for drunken teenagers. However, I have yet to hear of anybody being arrested. UNH housing is another story though. **Drinking in your room is grounds for eviction.** They're not kidding around."

Q "They are very strict about underage drinking on campus. At the beginning of the year they will make an example of you and **evict you from the dorm system on your first offense."**

Q "Campus police can be a pain in the butt, but just don't do anything stupid and you'll be fine. **There are plenty of arrests that happen every weekend** from drug or alcohol related problems, but only the silly people get caught. Just be responsible and you won't have to worry. Don't have open containers in the dorms or walk down the street after drinking, and you'll be fine. If you're being obvious and obnoxious you'll get in trouble. There are cops around frat row Thursday through Saturday nights, but there are fewer at the apartments."

Q "They handle it well. **RA's usually endure the initial contact** (offense)."

# The College Prowler Take On...
## Campus Strictness

The campus police don't seem to bother the students at UNH very much. As long as you are not acting like a fool, or putting yourself and others in danger you'll be given free reign over your activities on and around campus. Campus Police seem to realize that it is a college campus and they have to pick and choose their battles. Two things that campus police don't tolerate are drug offenses and underage drinking, especially in the dorms. Some local officers are even infamous for evicting students from the dorms on the first offense: all the more reason to drink intelligently and responsibly.

The Residential Life program is also very strict when it comes to dorm life, also evicting students for first time offenses if they are bad enough. Most of the time though, students are allowed a second chance. With incidents in the dorm there is a mandatory $50 charge for those who are caught drinking illegally. Due to the fact that UNH has been put under the microscope for recent problems including rioting after hockey games and other sporting events, the campus and local police have been much more present during certain high activity weekends. Overall, students at UNH can enjoy their college experiences if they are smart about their actions.

The College Prowler™ Grade on

### Campus Strictness: C-

A high Campus Strictness grade implies an overall lenient atmosphere; police and RAs are fairly tolerant, and the administration's rules are flexible.

*Clarification: A good grade means that campus strictness is not overwhelmingly present. The poorer the grade, the more strict the campus.*

# Parking

The Lowdown On...
## Parking

**UNH Parking Services:**
603-862-1010
295 MAST ROAD,
DURHAM, NH 03824
www.unh.edu/transportation/

**Student Parking Lot?**
Yes.

**Freshman Allowed to Park?**
No

**Approximate Parking Permit Cost:**
$100+ per year

## Common Parking Tickets:

Expired Meter: $15

No Parking Zone: $35

Handicapped Zone: $35

Fire Lane: Towing ($100)

## Best Places to Find a Parking Spot:

West Edge Parking lot

A-Lot

## Good Luck Getting a Parking Spot Here:

On the street before 6 p.m.

B-Lot

C-Lot

## Parking Permits

If you're a freshman, then don't try parking on-campus at UNH, it's as simple as that. You are not allowed to have a car on-campus and it is hard to talk the school into letting you have one. For upperclassmen, getting a permit is not hard if you register early and are content with what you get. The worst parking lot is West Edge, but that is only because it is about a mile of campus.

## Students Speak Out On...
# Parking

{ **"It's pretty tough to park here at UNH. The place where you're most likely to find a spot is in a remote lot (a bus ride away). Parking tickets are pretty common."**

Q "Parking is awful at UNH and it is **difficult to find a spot.**"

Q "**Parking is the only bad thing** about UNH. It can be a real pain sometimes."

Q "Parking is horrible. I have paid **over $500 in parking tickets.** If you don't have a pass you pretty much get screwed. There are parking meters, but they are usually all taken. The worst part about it is when they tow your car two minutes up the street and it costs you $85 to get it back."

Q "The parking situation has been an ongoing issue between the students, faculty, and the administration. They are talking about increasing prices to ridiculous amounts for spots, but **if you register early, you will have a spot somewhere.**"

Q "Campus parking is rough. You have to justify having a car as a freshman. You can have a car strictly if it is your only way of getting to school, or if you need to get to work. Many times you will have to **park your car away from the dorms and take a bus back into campus.**"

Q "There is no easy place to park during winter parking ban, but **parking is easy on the weekends** during regular season."

Q "It is **easy to park on campus**, but you must have a permit. As a freshman, they say no one is allowed to have a permit. My freshman friends found places to park, but at a high cost. Some of my friends **parked at a church for $200 a semester!"**

Q "Parking here sucks-don't bring your car. Getting tickets is expensive, costing from $30 to $50, and you have to pay or you don't graduate. Having a parking permit makes it easier to park, but you'll be stuck pretty far away. **Everything is in walking distance anyway**, and the buses are excellent."

Q "**Parking on campus is atrocious.** Sometimes commuters have to circle the parking lots waiting for a spot. People who live on campus and have a car must keep it in a lot, miles away. The University is making plans to fix this problem, perhaps by building garages, but this won't be complete for many years."

Q "It is **extremely difficult to find a parking space** if you arrive here after 8:30 in the morning."

Q "Parking is UNH's biggest problem. There are **plenty of spaces, but they are so far away!** If you are planning on living off campus and commuting, which I don't suggest doing as a freshman-parking lots are always fun! You have to get there almost a half an hour before class to take the shuttle to campus. During my junior and senior years I lived in Dover, which meant I had to drive to campus and find a parking spot every day. It really wasn't that bad-I had morning classes and if you get there early, there are plenty of spots. Come midday, you're fighting for spots. Parking isn't really a problem, but convenience of parking is. The school is so good, though, we all just deal with it and complain to feel better!"

# The College Prowler Take On...
# Parking

Parking is one of UNH's major problems that could use the administrations' attention. Students and faculty have fought over ticket prices, permit prices, and even plans for a new parking garage. Many students without parking permits have often had to take the trip to the pound and pay $85 just to get it back. Although it is unclear what the future will hold, the present situation leaves much to be desired. Students who manage to get a permit have to get to school early around 7:30 a.m. in order to get a parking spot within walking distance. After that, parking spots are only left in the West Edge lot which is a two minute bus ride away from campus.

Although getting close to campus is hard, finding a spot isn't. There is always a spot somewhere, whether in West Edge or not. During the weekends students can park in any lot on campus, but during the winter weekends a parking ban cancels out this privilege.

### The College Prowler™ Grade on
### Parking: C

A high grade in this section indicates that parking is both available and affordable, and that parking enforcement isn't overly severe.

# Transportation

### The Lowdown On...
## Transportation

## Ways to Get Around Town

**On Campus**

C&J Trailways
185 Grafton Drive
Portsmouth, NH 03801
1-800-258-7111

## Public Transportation:

C&J Trailways
185 Grafton Drive
Portsmouth, NH 03801
1-800-258-7111

## Car Rentals

Alamo
local: (412) 472-5060
national: (800) 327-9633
www.alamo.com

Avis
local: (412) 472-5200
national: (800) 831-2847
www.avis.com

Budget
local: (412) 472-5252
national: (800) 527-0700
www.budget.com

Dollar
local: (412) 472-5100
national: (800) 800-4000. www.
dollar.com

**(Car rentals, continued)**

Enterprise
local: (412) 472-3490
national: (800) 736-8222
www.enterprise.com

Hertz
local: (412) 472-5955
national: (800) 654-3131
www.hertz.com

National
local: (412) 472-5094
national: (800) 227-7368
www.nationalcar.com

## Airlines Serving Boston:

American Airlines
(800) 433-7300
www.americanairlines.com

Continental
(800) 523-3273
www.continental.com

Delta
(800) 221-1212
www.delta-air.com

Northwest
(800) 225-2525
www.nwa.com

Southwest
(800) 435-9792
www.southwest.com

TWA
(800) 221-2000
www.twa.com

United
(800) 241-6522
www.united.com

US Airways
(800) 428-4322
www.usairways.com

## Airport:

### Logan International Airport

http://www.massport.com/logan/
1-800-23-LOGAN

### How to Get There:

C&J Trailways
185 Grafton Drive
Portsmouth, NH 03801
1-800-258-7111

### A Cab Ride to the Airport

**Costs:** $150 for Logan International Airport

## Amtrak

The Amtrak station is right on campus. For scheduling information students must go to www.thedowneaster.com or call: 1-800-USA-RAIL.

## Travel Agents

University Travel Service
35 Main St.
Durham, NH
868-5970

## Students Speak Out On...
# Transportation

**"Transportation is definitely convenient. You can get to any town from UNH pretty easily."**

Q "The UNH Transportation system **is top-notch.**"

Q "They have **buses that go around campus** and stop at the main buildings, and they also have buses that go to the malls and Portsmouth. If you are really drunk, you can call Safe Rides and they will pick you up and drop you off. There is also a train that goes to Boston, which stops at the school."

Q "There are a lot of **buses to take you to surrounding towns**, and a lot of different routes too. Transportation is really good here."

Q "The **bus system is great**. It takes you to many different places other than Durham."

Q "UNH makes a **good effort to provide public transportation to its students**. Not only does it have a bus system that runs around the campus, it has buses that go to surrounding communities, like Dover, Newmarket, Newington, or Portsmouth. Generally, you can get a bus to the mall or downtown Portsmouth every hour. Also, the Downeaster, which runs from Portland to North Station in Boston, makes a stop right on our campus, which makes getting to Boston very easy."

Q "We have our own bus station. Buses go to Boston, the mall-**wherever you want to go.**"

Q "It is very **easy to get around campus and to the outly-ing towns** because of the transportation system."

Q "This is also **very convenient,** great for getting around campus, around town, and to surrounding communities."

Q "You can take the bus into a local town if you want, but it's definitely **nicer to have your own car.** There are also buses and a train that go to Boston, Maine, and other areas."

Q "Public Transportation comes often and takes you to the surrounding towns. There are buses to many things surrounding campus, such as grocery stores, the mall, the movies, and many other places. There are also many **on-campus shuttles** that bring you to different places on campus, which is helpful."

Q "The university has its own **bus system that you can take for free.** There are shuttles around campus and there are buses that take you to the mall, the movies, or nearby towns. There is a program called Safe Rides that you can call late at night-they take you if you have been drinking off-campus."

# The College Prowler Take On...
# Transportation

The shuttles around campus and to surrounding towns are usually efficient and on time. This is mostly due to the small size of Durham and the general area. Around campus, the only shuttle really needed is the West Edge parking lot shuttle. The worst time for buses is around four and five o' clock when most classes let out and the traffic is at its worst. This is when buses can get up to forty-five minutes late because there are no alternate roads to take.

To get out of town, transportation services run a route every hour out to surrounding towns. During the week this service goes until 10 p.m., but on the weekends the service stops running much earlier, so living off-campus can be an inconvenience. To get to Logan International Airport, the best way is to have a friend drive you because the drive is about an hour. If you can't find a ride, the train that goes right through Durham runs several times per day for about $12 one way. There is also the C and J Trailways as a means of transportation.

**The College Prowler™ Grade on**

**Transportation: B+**

A high grade for Transportation indicates that campus buses, public buses, cabs, and rental cars are readily-available and affordable. Other determining factors include proximity to an airport and the necessity of transportation.

# Weather

### The Lowdown On...
## Weather

| Average Temperature | | Average Precipitation | |
| --- | --- | --- | --- |
| Fall: | 61-40°F | Fall: | 4.06in. |
| Winter: | 35-16°F | Winter: | 3.13in. |
| Spring: | 60-34°F | Spring: | 4.09in. |
| Summer: | 80-55°F | Summer: | 3.32in. |

## Students Speak Out On...
# Weather

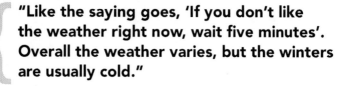

**"Like the saying goes, 'If you don't like the weather right now, wait five minutes'. Overall the weather varies, but the winters are usually cold."**

Q "The weather in New Hampshire can get **very warm and very cold.**"

Q "It's **pretty nice at the beginning of the year,** like in the seventies or eighties. I wear shorts or capris most days, but then winter comes and it's chilly! You'll need hats, mittens, and a winter jacket. I hope you like snow! The end of the year is really nice, too. It can get up to around seventy to eighty degrees and we had some days around the nineties. These are the days that we hit up the beach, which is about twenty minutes away!"

Q "The weather is hot and sunny in the summer, cold and windy in the winter, and **lots of snow.**"

Q "It is New Hampshire, and the weather does get pretty cold but, at the same time, it can be fun. We usually have snow from November or December until March, but there are **lots of winter sports and activities in the area.**"

Q "Since we are **right near the beach,** there is always a breeze. It is hot at the beginning and at the end of the year, and usually pretty humid-the winters suck. We get a load of snow and it is a hassle getting to class."

Q "Be **prepared for everything and anything;** you're in New Hampshire after all."

Q "The weather is different, that's for sure. It will be hot and humid at first, but it cools down quickly and we get lots of snow and rain. **New England weather is crazy** sometimes."

Q "We have the typical New England, **four-season weather.** It gets pretty cold and snowy from November to March, so remember the sweaters and tube socks. But in September and May, we are pretty close to the beach, which is nice. Remember the flip-flops."

Q "Weather can be cold in the long dark winter, but awesome in the spring and early fall. **Bring clothes for all seasons** typical of New England."

Q "The **weather in New Hampshire always changes.** At the beginning of the year you'll need to bring your shorts and tank tops, but as it gets to be winter, make sure you bring your boots and scarves because it gets really cold. If you ski, make sure you don't forget your ski equipment! Around March it starts warming up again, so go home during spring break and get your shorts again. Don't forget a bathing suit and towel, too. There is a beach nearby."

Q "Umm, it is **winter here like half the year.** You'll need a thick jacket, boots, scarf, hat, mittens, long johns, etc.."

# The College Prowler Take On...
# Weather

UNH is in the heart of New England, and that means the weather changes about every five minutes. There is absolutely no consistency in the climate here. It's kind of like Mother Natures' little freak experiment. UNH gets the best and the worst of every season, so bring a little bit of everything. Students normally agree that the best season is usually the fall with the leaves turning beautiful colors and the weather being mostly stable. However, many beach-goers will disagree and say that summer is the best season because of the close proximity of the coast. You can usually get away with a t-shirt and shorts just about every day of the fall. During the summer months, many UNH students take advantage of the beaches nearby. The warmer weather allows them to frequently do so.

In the winter, each year brings different amounts of snow. On average, the campus sees a moderate one or two feet of snow, so don't be afraid to bring your snow gear to play in. In spring, the campus is drowned in mud, but the temperatures usually allow you to break out the lighter clothes once again. Although you will need a varying degree of clothing to keep you comfortable around campus, the weather is usually right in the middle of the spectrum.

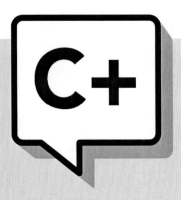

**The College Prowler™ Grade on**

**Weather: C+**

A high Weather grade designates that temperatures are mild and rarely reach extremes, that the campus tends to be sunny rather than rainy, and that weather is fairly consistent rather than unpredictable.

# Report Card Summary

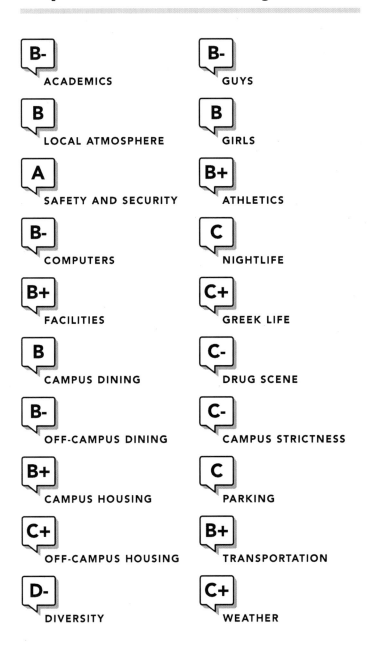

**B-** ACADEMICS

**B** LOCAL ATMOSPHERE

**A** SAFETY AND SECURITY

**B-** COMPUTERS

**B+** FACILITIES

**B** CAMPUS DINING

**B-** OFF-CAMPUS DINING

**B+** CAMPUS HOUSING

**C+** OFF-CAMPUS HOUSING

**D-** DIVERSITY

**B-** GUYS

**B** GIRLS

**B+** ATHLETICS

**C** NIGHTLIFE

**C+** GREEK LIFE

**C-** DRUG SCENE

**C-** CAMPUS STRICTNESS

**C** PARKING

**B+** TRANSPORTATION

**C+** WEATHER

# Overall Experience

Students Speak Out On...
## Overall Experience

**"I absolutely love it here and wouldn't have it any other way. That's why I came all the way from Seattle to go here."**

Q "My overall experience has been awesome. I **wouldn't dream of leaving."**

Q "I was accepted to all the schools I applied to, but I chose UNH because it was the one I could afford. To be honest, it wasn't my first choice. Let me tell you, though, that I had a great time while I was there. **The school is wonderful** and I had a good time."

Q "If I had to sum up UNH in a few words, I think it would be **'party school'."**

Q "I love it here and I wouldn't go somewhere else if I was offered a full scholarship. **It's awesome here."**

Q "I am very pleased with my decision to attend that school. The **campus is just so pretty, calm and laid-back,** and everything is at your disposal. UNH really gives students a chance to shape their own experiences. Classes, parties, friends, drugs, sororities-they are all there for you to mold into whatever you want. Nothing is forced in your face; it all just floats around your head like puzzle pieces, and it is your job to put that puzzle together."

Q "At first I was unsure of coming to UNH because I live so close. Once I got the chance to meet people and get to know the campus I was hooked. **The people make it great here."**

Q "There are **times that the university makes you feel more like a number than a person,** and the business aspect of the school can be overpowering. You definitely know the administration is out to make as much money as possible, but the school overall is wonderful"

Q "I had a lot of **trouble adjusting to college life my freshman year,** as a lot of students do. But after being here for two years, I have come to love UNH as my home. All of the experiences that I've had here have helped me to grow as a person, and I'm sure that UNH will provide me with many more. The people here are great; the students are so down-to-earth. When it comes down to it, I can't imagine myself anywhere other than here."

Q "For originally a safety school, I feel that UNH was without a doubt **the best choice for me."**

Q "When the winter weather gets awful, I wish I had chosen a school in Florida. Other than that, **I am happy with my school experience so far."**

Q "UNH has been awesome to me, **getting involved with different things definitely helps.** There is so much to do here, and so many opportunities to be taken advantage of. I am glad I decided to come here and couldn't be happier with my choice."

Q "I hear a lot of people complaining that UNH is kind of a boring school, but **I don't ever really have a problem finding plenty of things to do.** Plus, the people are all awesome here."

Q "I have loved it at UNH. I had an amazing freshman year, and even though I hated the beginning of my sophomore year, I ended up loving it because I went abroad to London my second semester. **UNH has many abroad programs** and it was the greatest part of my UNH experience. This year was awesome. I really got involved, loved my classes, and had an awesome time with my friends. I write a column for the school newspaper, I'm in a theatre troupe, I was in a play this past semester, and I am always doing things on campus. The best advice I can give you, no matter what school you choose, is to get involved. You meet the most people this way and keep busy."

# The College Prowler Take On...
# Overall Experience

Most students did not choose UNH as their first choice. Some felt wary because they felt that UNH was too close to home, others because the school was too far away. However, many of these same students will tell you that they learned to appreciate UNH and its well rounded course curriculum, spectacular seasons, local "college town" atmosphere, and myriad of activities for students of all ages. It's safe to say that UNH is a school that caters to the needs of many different personalities. The campus also encourages students to explore all that they have to offer through many different organizations including the American Students Association, several fraternities and sororities, and The National Society of Minorities in Hospitality. Although sometimes the campus has its shortcomings in some areas, the effort of the administration is greatly evident through recent renovations of several dormitories (Mills, Congreve) and on-campus facilities (Holloway Commons, Whittemore Center). A very open and accepting environment seems to carry over to the non-student residents of Durham as well. This seems obvious due to the amount of specials by local businesses geared toward UNH students. I seriously doubt if The Durham House of Pizza would sell many one-dollar slices of pizza after midnight if it weren't for the students.

The town of Durham revolves around the students and vice-versa. Most students will agree that just about everyone they meet on campus has a great personality and are, not to mention, very good looking. This atmosphere provides a very comforting and safe campus that genuinely leaves the college experience up to the students to mold.

# The Inside Scoop

**The Lowdown On...**
## The Inside Scoop

### UNH Slang:

Know the slang, know the school. The following is a list of things you really need to know before coming to UNH. The more of these words you know, the better off you'll be.

**The MUB:** The Memorial Union Building. This is the main student center on campus.

**The Whitt:** The Whittemore Center, which houses the hockey rink and the student athletic center.

**PCAC:** Paul Creative Arts Center. This is home to the Art Majors.

**Webcat:** The schools online network for registering for classes, checking grades and other personal information.

**CampCo:** The Campus Convenience store.

**24:** the convenience store 24.

**Fireplace room:** A room in the MUB where students mainly sleep on couches.

**T-Hall lawn:** the lawn in front of Thompson Hall that is home to numerous lounging students in the spring.

**Boulder Field:** A field on campus property that has a giant boulder in the middle of it. This is also the unofficial campus Frisbee field.

**The DUMP:** The local grocery store also known as the Durham Market Place.

**Zylas:** The P.K. Zylas store where you can find just about anything you will ever need in college life.

**The Greens:** A group of apartments on Madbury street, where weekend parties are very frequent.

**The Ghetto:** A group of apartment notorious for being very cheap and very dirty to say the least.

**Frat Row:** Also known as Madbury Road, and is where all the Fraternity and Sorority houses are found.

**Kurt's Lunch Box:** The guy who sells late night snacks and sandwiches out of a trailer which can be found behind Mills Hall.

**College Woods:** The area of woods behind the athletic fields, and Boulder field.

## School Spirit

UNH school spirit is strong in areas such as sports. UNH's biggest team is the Men's Hockey team. They have made it to numerous Division I final fours and a few championship games. This high caliber team brings out the heckler in everyone. The UNH fans are regarded as some the harshest fans in college hockey. Original cheers include much profanity, sexuality, and personal attacks on opposing teams and their fans. However, the fans do it all for their team and hold much pride in them win or lose. Outside of sports, UNH pride is fairly strong. Students here generally seem proud to be a Wildcat. Everyone owns at least one UNH sweatshirt, and lives in it through the winter months.

## Traditions

At the Men's Hockey games there are many traditions, the most popular is throwing a dead fish onto the ice after the first goal of every home game.

White-out the Whitt is a hockey tradition where fans wear white to one of the men's hockey home games.

Boulderfest is the UNH version of Woodstock. Activities include all day Frisbee, music, food and a huge bonfire. This event happens every year as an end of the year celebration.

Stoke Wreath Lighting is a tradition where the Stoke Hall staff constructs a giant wreath out of pine bows and Christmas lights and hangs it from the building with a crane. There is a ceremony to officially light up the wreath, where warm food and music kick off the holiday spirit.

## Things I Wish I Knew Before Coming to UNH

• Walking ten miles a day is something you better get used to.

• Ultimate Frisbee means more to some people than life itself.

• The 4th floor of the library has the most comfortable chairs to read in.

• Find anyway possible to bring your car to school.

• Laundry baskets make great sleds.

• Sprint is the only cell phone service that works in this area. Period.

## Tips to Succeed at UNH

- Work really hard your first year to get your GPA up high, because it's incredibly hard to raise it once it goes down.

- Meet with your professors and get to know them well and you will always do better than if you didn't.

- It's a good idea to know what you want to study by the end of sophomore year.

- Join all the student groups you can in your freshman year and find people that you really have a connection with.

- Don't take 8 a.m. classes, you will never go to them.

- Buy your books a week early.

## UNH Urban Legends

- Congreve Hall is supposedly haunted by the ghost of a student from early 1900s.

- Stoke Hall, a dorm, was supposedly constructed to be easily demolished with dynamite.

- It is said that if you do the deed with a special someone in the old wagon on top of Wagon Hill before you graduate, you will have good luck for the rest of your life. You also have to stay there overnight.

# Finding a Job or Internship

The Lowdown On...
## Finding a Job or Internship

### Career Center Resources & Services:

Jobline
W.O.R.K. (wildcat online recruiting kit)
Job fairs
Internships
On-campus recruiting
Career mentor network

### Firms That Most Frequently Hire Graduates:

Raytheon
Sun Life Financial
Libery Mutual
Philip Morris
John Hancock

The best way to find an internship at UNH is through your major. Many of the majors offer senior internships for credit. Some internships are paid, and most are required. The UNH career center departments take great pride in setting students up with numerous job opportunities. Students also are assigned an advisor in their specific major who can provide the best help with internships in the students' particular major. The campus also holds numerous job fairs for specific majors as well, which are open to anyone in those majors, and provide direct contact with employers. The career center is located in Hood House next to the MUB.

## Advice

Have a good idea of what you want to study before you get to UNH. The sooner you know the sooner you can start planning and talking with your advisor. This also gives you plenty of time to explore options. Most importantly, don't worry; it's not the end of the world if you don't know how to plan your life right off the bat. It is better to take the time to find out what you really want in life.

# Alumni

**The Lowdown On...**
## Alumni

**Website:**
http://www.unh.edu/alumni/index.html

**Office:**
Elliott Alumni Center
9 Edgewood Road
Durham, NH 03824-1987
(603) 862-2040

**Services Available:**
Travel Tours
Legacy Program
Honors and Awards
ISU Credit Cards
Insurance Programs
Alumni Mentor Program
ISU Clubs
Career Services for Alumni
Scholarships (for future and current students)

## Major Alumni Events:
Homing

Reunion

## Famous UO Alumni:
Mike O'Malley - star of the Nickelodeon show 'Guts' and the ABC show 'Yes Dear'.

## Alumni Publications:
UNH Magazine

UNH Magazine Online

Alumni Monthly

UNH Connection

The Alumni House (Elliot Center) is located near the Woodside student apartments behind the Whittemore Center. It has meeting rooms and banquet rooms that are catered frequently by the UHS Catering Service. The mission of the UNH Alumni Association is to advocate for the University of New Hampshire and its alumni, and promote the University's historic land-grant mission of teaching, research and public service. Through its programs and services, the Alumni Association develops a spirit of loyalty to the University, engaging and serving alumni, student, parents, faculty, and the public.

# Student Organizations

Accounting Students' Association

Alpha Chi Sigma

American Advertising Federation (AAF)

American Sign Language Club

American Society of Civil Engineers

American Society of Mechanical Engineers

Chinese Students and Scholars Association

Collegiate FFA Chapter

Earth Science Club

Engineers Without Borders

Eta Sigma Phi

Future Marine Officers Association

Golden Key National Honor Society

Graduate Business Club

Marketing Club

Mock Trial Club

Music Education National Conference

National Society of Collegiate Scholars

National Society of Minorities in Hospitality

National Student Speech, Language, Hearing Association

Organization of Future Physician Assistants

Pre-Vet Club

Psychology Club

Ranger Club

Recreation Management and Policy Association

Society of Women Engineers

→

Student Health Management Organization

Student Occupational Therapy Association

WSBE Greeks

American Cancer Society Walk for Life

Alpha Phi Omega

Circle K International

Cool-Aid

Students Advocating Gender Equality

Tau Beta Phi

ZXP Community Action

Alabaster Blue

Anime Club

Artists' Circle

Brothers & Sisters in Step

Campus Activities Board

Hep Cats Swing Club

Juggling Club

Kappa Kappa Psi

Mask and Dagger Theatrical Society

Memorial Union Student Organization

New Hampshire Gentlemen

New Hampshire Notables

Not Too Sharp

ODA Entertainment

Perfect Fifth

Student Com. on Popular Entertainment

Student Motion Picture Association

Theatre Sports

Weekend Wildcats

WildACT

Wildcat Marching Band

Black Student Union

Brazilian Student Organization

Chinese Student Organization

Diversity Support Coalition

French Club

Hillel

Indian Student Association

Japanese Club

MOSAICO

Native American Cultural Association

United Asian Coalition (UAC)

Memorial Union Board of Governors

Student Senate

College Democrats

College Republicans

Democracy Matters

Generation Dean

Student Environmental Action Coalition

UNH for Clark

UNH for Kerry

# The Best &
# The Worst

## The Ten **BEST** Things About UNH:

| | |
|---|---|
| 1 | The Men's Hockey Team |
| 2 | Outdoor barbeques |
| 3 | The country scenery |
| 4 | The ocean beaches |
| 5 | $1 pizza |
| 6 | Thompson hall lawn on a warm spring day |
| 7 | Broomball competitions |
| 8 | Kurt's Lunch Box |
| 9 | Smoothies from the coffee shop |
| 10 | The "On The Spot" column in the student newspaper |

# The Ten WORST Things About UNH:

| | |
|---|---|
| **1** | The bell tower that rings every thirty minutes |
| **2** | Parking |
| **3** | The lack of Holidays |
| **4** | Mud season |
| **5** | The wind |
| **6** | Traffic on Main Street |
| **7** | The confusing layout of Holloway Commons |
| **8** | Winter-parking ban |
| **9** | The price of books at the UNH Bookstore |
| **10** | The new meal plans |

# Visiting UNH

The Lowdown On...
## Visiting UNH

## HOTEL INFORMATION

**The New England Conference Center**
15 Strafford Ave. UNH
Durham, NH
862-2801
Distance from Campus: On Campus
Price Range: $134 - $145

**The Three Chimneys Inn**
17 Newmarket Road
Durham, NH
868-7800
Distance from Campus: ¼ mile
Price range: $120 - $200 The TheThe The DIRECTIONS TO CAMPUS

## Take a Campus Virtual Tour:

www.unh.edu/admissions

## To Schedule a Group
## Information Session or Interview:

From: 10:30 a.m. - 1 p.m. Monday through Friday

Call: (603) 862- 1360

The admissions staff interviews Monday through Friday, but interviews will not be held in the month of May.

## Campus Tours:

Tours are at 10:30 a.m. and 1 p.m. except for holidays and a few weeks in the end of May.

## Overnight Vists:

The only overnight visits that are available are through Athletic teams and the orientation program for freshmen during the summer

# Directions to Campus

### From Concord, NH:

Take Route 4 East to the 155A exit. Follow directions as listed from Boston. (Driving time, approx. 45 minutes)

Driving from the South:

### From Boston, MA:

Take I-95 North to Exit 4 (NH Lakes and Mountains, Spaulding Turnpike). Continue North to Exit 6W and follow Route 4 West. Exit at Route 155A and turn east toward Durham. Follow 155A through a short stretch of fields to the UNH campus. (driving time, approx. 90 minutes)

Driving from the East:

### From Portland, MN:

Follow I-95 South to Exit 5. Continue on Spaulding Turnpike North to Exit 6W and follow Route 4 West. Follow directions as listed from Boston. (Driving time, approx. 60 minutes)

### From Manchester, NH:

Take Route 101 to Epping; go north on Route 125 to the Lee Traffic Circle. Drive East on Route 4 to the Route 155A exit. Follow directions as listed from Boston. (Driving time, approx. 45 minutes)

# Words to Know

**Academic Probation** – A student can receive this if they fail to keep up with their school's academic minimums. Those who are unable to improve their grades after receiving this warning can possibly face dismissal.

**Beer Pong / Beirut** – A drinking game with numerous cups of beer arranged in a particular pattern on each side of a table. The goal is to get a ping pong ball into one of the opponent's cups by throwing the ball or hitting it with a paddle. If the ball lands in a cup, the opponent is required to drink the beer.

**Bid** – An invitation from a fraternity or sorority to pledge their specific house.

**Blue-Light Phone** – Brightly-colored phone posts with a blue light bulb on top. These phones exist for security purposes and are located at various outside locations around most campuses. If a student has an emergency or is feeling endangered, they can pick up one of these phones (free of charge) to connect with campus police or an escort service.

**Campus Police** – Policemen who are specifically assigned to a given institution. Campus police are not regular city officers; they are employed by the university in a full-time capacity.

**Club Sports** – A level of sports that falls somewhere between varsity and intramural. If a student is unable to commit to a varsity team but has a lot of passion for athletics, a club sport could be a better, less intense option. If a club sport still requires too much commitment, intramurals often involve no traveling and a lot less time.

**Cocaine** – An illegal drug. Also known as "coke" or "blow," cocaine often resembles a white crystalline or powdery substance. It is highly addictive and dangerous.

**Common Application** – An application that students can use to apply to multiple schools.

**Course Registration** – The time when a student selects what courses they would like for the upcoming quarter or semester. Prior to registration, it is best to have an idea of several back-up courses in case a particular class becomes full. If a course is full, a student can place themselves on the waitlist, although this still does not guarantee entry.

**Division Athletics** – Athletics range from Division I to Division III. Division IA is the most competitive, while Division III is considered to be the least competitive.

**Dorm** – Short for dormitory, a dorm is an on-campus housing facility. Dorms can provide a range of options from suite-style rooms to more communal options that include shared bathrooms. Most first-year students live in dorms. Some upperclassmen who wish to stay on campus also choose this option.

**Early Action** – A way to apply to a school and get an early acceptance response without a binding commitment. This is a system that is becoming less and less available.

**Early Decision** – An option that students should use only if they are positive that a place is their dream school. If a student applies to a school using the early decision option and is admitted, they are required and bound to attend that university. Admission rates are usually higher with early decision students because the school knows that a student is making them their first choice.

**Ecstasy** – An illegal drug. Also known as "E" or "X," ecstasy looks like a pill and most resembles an aspirin. Considered a party drug, ecstasy is very dangerous and can be deadly.

**Ethernet** – An extremely fast internet connection that is usually available in most university-owned residence halls. To use an Ethernet connection properly, a student will need a network card and cable for their computer.

**Fake ID** – A counterfeit identification card that contains false information. Most commonly, students get fake IDs and change their birthdates so that they appear to be older than 21 (of legal drinking age). Even though it is illegal, many college students have fake IDs in hopes of purchasing alcohol or getting into bars.

**Frosh** – Slang for "freshmen."

**Hazing** – Initiation rituals that must be completed for membership into some fraternities or sororities. Numerous universities have outlawed hazing due to its degrading or dangerous requirements.

**Sports (IMs)** – A popular, and usually free, student activity where students create teams and compete against other groups for fun. These sports vary in competitiveness and can include a range of activities—everything from billiards to water polo. IM sports are a great way to meet people with similar interests.

**Keg** – Officially called a half barrel, a keg contains roughly 200 12-ounce servings of beer and is often found at college parties.

**LSD** – An illegal drug. Also known as acid, this hallucinogenic drug most commonly resembles a tab of paper.

**Marijuana** – An illegal drug. Also known as weed or pot; besides alcohol, marijuana is one of the most commonly-found drugs on campuses across the country.

**Major** –The focal point of a student's college studies; a specific topic that is studied for a degree. Examples of majors include physics, English, history, computer science, economics, business, and music. Many students decide on a specific major before arriving on campus, while others are simply "undecided" and figure it out later. Those who are extremely interested in two areas can also choose to double major.

**Meal Block** – The equivalent of one meal. Students on a "meal plan" usually receive a fixed number of meals per week.

Each meal, or "block," can be redeemed at the school's dining facilities in place of cash. More often than not, if a student fails to use their weekly allotment of meal blocks, they will be forfeited.

**Minor** – An additional focal point in a student's education. Often serving as a compliment or addition to a student's main area of focus, a minor has fewer requirements and prerequisites to fulfill than a major. Minors are not required for graduation from most schools; however some students who want to further explore many different interests choose to have both a major and a minor.

**Mushrooms** – An illegal drug. Also known as "shrooms," this drug looks like regular mushrooms but are extremely hallucinogenic.

**Off-Campus Housing** – Housing from a particular landlord or rental group that is not affiliated with the university. Depending on the college, off-campus housing can range from extremely popular to non-existent. Those students who choose to live off campus are typically given more freedom, but they also have to deal with things such as possible subletting scenarios, furniture, and bills. In addition to these factors, rental prices and distance often affect a student's decision to move off campus.

**Office Hours** – Time that teachers set aside for students who have questions about the coursework. Office hours are a good place for students to go over any problems and to show interest in the subject material.

**Pledging** – The time after a student has gone through rush, received a bid, and has chosen a particular fraternity or sorority they would like to join. Pledging usually lasts anywhere from one to two semesters. Once the pledging period is complete and a particular student has done everything that is required to become a member, they are considered a brother or sister. If a fraternity or a sorority would decide to "haze" a group of students, these initiation rituals would take place during the pledging period.

**Private Institution** – A school that does not use taxpayers dollars to help subsidize education costs. Private schools typically cost more than public schools and are usually smaller.

**Prof** – Slang for "professor."

**Public Institution** – A school that uses taxpayers dollars to help subsidize education costs. Public schools are often a good value for in-state residents and tend to be larger than most private colleges.

**Quarter System** (sometimes referred to as the Trimester System) – A type of academic calendar system. In this setup, students take classes for three academic periods. The first quarter usually starts in late September or early October and concludes right before Christmas. The second quarter usually starts around early to mid–January and finishes up around March or April. The last quarter, or "third quarter," usually starts in late March or early April and finishes up in late May or Mid-June. The fourth quarter is summer. The major difference between the quarter system and semester system is that students take more courses but with less coverage.

**RA** (Resident Assistant) – A student leader who is assigned to a particular floor in a dormitory in order to help to the other students who live there. A RA's duties include ensuring student safety and providing guidance or assistance wherever possible.

**Recitation** – An extension of a specific course; a "review" session of sorts. Because some classes are so large, recitations offer a setting with fewer students where students can ask questions and get help from professors or TAs in a more personalized environment. As a result, it is common for most large lecture classes to be supplemented with recitations.

**Rolling Admissions** – A form of admissions. Most commonly found at public institutions, schools with this type of policy continue to accept students throughout the year until their class sizes are met. For example, some schools begin accepting students as early as December and will continue to do so until April or May.

**Room and Board** – This is typically the combined cost of a university-owned room and a meal plan.

**Room Draw/Housing Lottery** – A common way to pick on-campus room assignments for the following year. If a student decides to remain in university-owned housing, they are assigned a unique number that, along with seniority, is used to choose their new rooms for the next year.

**Rush** – The period in which students can meet the brothers and sisters of a particular chapter and find out if a given fraternity or sorority is right for them. Rushing a fraternity or a sorority is not a requirement at any school. The goal of rush is to give students who are serious about pledging a feel for what to expect.

**Semester System** – The most common type of academic calendar system at college campuses. This setup typically includes two semesters in a given school year. The "fall" semester starts around the end of August or early September and finishes right before winter vacation. The "spring" semester usually starts in mid-January and ends around late April or May.

**Student Center/Rec Center/Student Union** – A common area on campus that often contains study areas, recreation facilities, and eateries. This building is often a good place to meet up with fellow students and is most commonly used as a hangout. Depending on the school, the student center can have a huge role or a non-existent role in campus life.

**Student ID** – A university-issued photo ID that serves as a student's key to many different functions within an institution. Some schools require students to show these cards in order to get into dorms, libraries, cafeterias, and other facilities. In addition to storing meal plan information, in some cases, a student ID can actually work as a debit card and allow students to purchase things from bookstores or local shops.

**Suite** – A type of dorm room. Unlike other places that have communal bathrooms that are shared by the entire floor, a suite has a private bathroom. Suite-style dorm rooms can house anywhere from two to ten students.

**TA** (Teacher's Assistant) – An undergraduate or grad student who helps in some manner with a specific course. In some cases, a TA will teach a class, assist a professor, grade assignments, or conduct office hours.

**Undergraduate** – A student who is in the process of studying for their Bachelor (college) degree.

## ABOUT THE AUTHOR:

My name is Jeff Lewis and although I wish to bring peace to the world I realize that I'm probably best off settling for just having a good time and enjoying the rest of my college career at UNH.

I was born and raised in Holderness, NH, near Plymouth State College. Before you ask, I didn't go to Plymouth State College because, honestly, that is just a little too close to home. I thought UNH would be a better fit because of its size and variety of courses. I am currently pursing a major in journalism and just enjoying everyday as it comes to me.

I particularly enjoyed writing this guidebook because I believe students should know the truth about the schools they are looking at. I also hope I helped students answer any questions they had about UNH and possibly raised their interest in the school, because I believe UNH has a lot to offer to students who are not sure what direction they want to go in life. In parting, live life to the fullest and never stop exploring.


Sincerely,

Jeff Lewis


Email the author at jefflewis@collegeprowler.com

# Notes

......................................................................

......................................................................

......................................................................

......................................................................

......................................................................

......................................................................

......................................................................

......................................................................

......................................................................

......................................................................

......................................................................

......................................................................

......................................................................

# Notes

........................................................................

........................................................................

........................................................................

........................................................................

........................................................................

........................................................................

........................................................................

........................................................................

........................................................................

........................................................................

........................................................................

........................................................................

........................................................................

........................................................................

# Notes

......................................................

......................................................

......................................................

......................................................

......................................................

......................................................

......................................................

......................................................

......................................................

......................................................

......................................................

......................................................

......................................................

# Notes

........................................................................

........................................................................

........................................................................

........................................................................

........................................................................

........................................................................

........................................................................

........................................................................

........................................................................

........................................................................

........................................................................

........................................................................

........................................................................

# Notes

....................................................................

....................................................................

....................................................................

....................................................................

....................................................................

....................................................................

....................................................................

....................................................................

....................................................................

....................................................................

....................................................................

....................................................................

....................................................................

....................................................................

# Notes

....................................................................

....................................................................

....................................................................

....................................................................

....................................................................

....................................................................

....................................................................

....................................................................

....................................................................

....................................................................

....................................................................

....................................................................

....................................................................

# Notes

..................................................................................

..................................................................................

..................................................................................

..................................................................................

..................................................................................

..................................................................................

..................................................................................

..................................................................................

..................................................................................

..................................................................................

..................................................................................

..................................................................................

..................................................................................

# Notes

......................................................................
......................................................................
......................................................................
......................................................................
......................................................................
......................................................................
......................................................................
......................................................................
......................................................................
......................................................................
......................................................................
......................................................................
......................................................................

# Notes

..................................................................

..................................................................

..................................................................

..................................................................

..................................................................

..................................................................

..................................................................

..................................................................

..................................................................

..................................................................

..................................................................

..................................................................

..................................................................

# Notes

..................................................................

..................................................................

..................................................................

..................................................................

..................................................................

..................................................................

..................................................................

..................................................................

..................................................................

..................................................................

..................................................................

..................................................................

..................................................................

# Notes

....................................................................

....................................................................

....................................................................

....................................................................

....................................................................

....................................................................

....................................................................

....................................................................

....................................................................

....................................................................

....................................................................

....................................................................

....................................................................

# Notes

..................................................................

..................................................................

..................................................................

..................................................................

..................................................................

..................................................................

..................................................................

..................................................................

..................................................................

..................................................................

..................................................................

..................................................................

..................................................................

# Notes

..............................................................

..............................................................

..............................................................

..............................................................

..............................................................

..............................................................

..............................................................

..............................................................

..............................................................

..............................................................

..............................................................

..............................................................

..............................................................

# Notes

..................................................................
..................................................................
..................................................................
..................................................................
..................................................................
..................................................................
..................................................................
..................................................................
..................................................................
..................................................................
..................................................................
..................................................................
..................................................................

# Notes

........................................................

........................................................

........................................................

........................................................

........................................................

........................................................

........................................................

........................................................

........................................................

........................................................

........................................................

........................................................

........................................................

# Notes

....................................................................

....................................................................

....................................................................

....................................................................

....................................................................

....................................................................

....................................................................

....................................................................

....................................................................

....................................................................

....................................................................

....................................................................

....................................................................

# Notes

....................................................................

....................................................................

....................................................................

....................................................................

....................................................................

....................................................................

....................................................................

....................................................................

....................................................................

....................................................................

....................................................................

....................................................................

....................................................................

....................................................................

# Notes

........................................................

........................................................

........................................................

........................................................

........................................................

........................................................

........................................................

........................................................

........................................................

........................................................

........................................................

........................................................

........................................................

........................................................

# Notes

......................................................

......................................................

......................................................

......................................................

......................................................

......................................................

......................................................

......................................................

......................................................

......................................................

......................................................

......................................................

......................................................

# Need More Help?

Do you have more questions about this school? Can't find a certain statistic? College Prowler is here to help. We are the best source of college information on the planet. We have a network of thousands of students who can get the latest information on any school to you ASAP. E-mail us at *info@collegeprowler.com* with your college-related questions. It's like having an older sibling show you the ropes!

**Email Us Your College-Related Questions!**

Check out **www.collegeprowler.com** for more details.
1.800.290.2682

# Notes

....................................................................

....................................................................

....................................................................

....................................................................

....................................................................

....................................................................

....................................................................

....................................................................

....................................................................

....................................................................

....................................................................

....................................................................

....................................................................

# Tell Us What Life Is Really Like At Your School!

Have you ever wanted to let people know what your school is really like? Now's your chance to help millions of high school students choose the right school.

**Let your voice be heard and win cash and prizes!**

Check out **www.collegeprowler.com** for more info!

# Notes

....................................................................

....................................................................

....................................................................

....................................................................

....................................................................

....................................................................

....................................................................

....................................................................

....................................................................

....................................................................

....................................................................

....................................................................

....................................................................

# Do You Have What It Takes To Get Admitted?

The College Prowler Road to College Counseling Program is here. An admissions officer will review your candidacy at the school of your choice and create a 12+ page personal admission plan. We rate your credentials with the same criteria used by school admissions committees. We assess your strengths and weaknesses and create a plan of action that makes a difference.

Check out **www.collegeprowler.com** or call 1.800.290.2682 for complete details.

# Notes

....................................................................

....................................................................

....................................................................

....................................................................

....................................................................

....................................................................

....................................................................

....................................................................

....................................................................

....................................................................

....................................................................

....................................................................

....................................................................

# Pros and Cons

Still can't figure out if this is the right school for you?
You've already read through this in-depth guide; why not
list the pros and cons? It will really help with narrowing down
your decision and determining whether or not
this school is right for you.

| Pros | Cons |
| --- | --- |
|  |  |
|  |  |
|  |  |
|  |  |
|  |  |
|  |  |
|  |  |
|  |  |
|  |  |
|  |  |
|  |  |
|  |  |
|  |  |
|  |  |

# Notes

..................................................................

..................................................................

..................................................................

..................................................................

..................................................................

..................................................................

..................................................................

..................................................................

..................................................................

..................................................................

..................................................................

..................................................................

..................................................................

# Notes

........................................................

........................................................

........................................................

........................................................

........................................................

........................................................

........................................................

........................................................

........................................................

........................................................

........................................................

........................................................

........................................................

# Get Paid To Rep Your City!

## *Make money for college!*

**Earn cash by telling your friends about College Prowler!**

**Excellent Pay + Incentives + Bonuses**

**Compete with reps across the nation for cash bonuses**

**Gain marketing and communication skills**

**Build your resume and gain work experience for future career opportunities**

**Flexible work hours; make your own schedule**

**Opportunities for advancement**

Contact *sales@collegeprowler.com*
Apply now at **www.collegeprowler.com**

# Notes

..................................................................

..................................................................

..................................................................

..................................................................

..................................................................

..................................................................

..................................................................

..................................................................

..................................................................

..................................................................

..................................................................

..................................................................

..................................................................

# Notes

..................................................................

..................................................................

..................................................................

..................................................................

..................................................................

..................................................................

..................................................................

..................................................................

..................................................................

..................................................................

..................................................................

..................................................................

..................................................................

# Notes

......................................................................

......................................................................

......................................................................

......................................................................

......................................................................

......................................................................

......................................................................

......................................................................

......................................................................

......................................................................

......................................................................

......................................................................

......................................................................

# Write For Us!
## *Get Published! Voice Your Opinion.*

Writing a College Prowler guidebook is both fun and rewarding; our open-ended format allows your own creativity free reign. Our writers have been featured in national newspapers and have seen their names in bookstores across the country. Now is your chance to break into the publishing industry with one of the country's fastest-growing publishers!

Apply now at **www.collegeprowler.com**

Contact *editor@collegeprowler.com* or
call 1.800.290.2682 for more details.

# Tell Us What Life Is Really Like At Your School!

Have you ever wanted to let people know what your school is really like? Now's your chance to help millions of high school students choose the right school.

**Let your voice be heard and win cash and prizes!**

Check out **www.collegeprowler.com** for more info!

# Notes

........................................................

........................................................

........................................................

........................................................

........................................................

........................................................

........................................................

........................................................

........................................................

........................................................

........................................................

........................................................

........................................................

........................................................

# Do You Have What It Takes To Get Admitted?

The College Prowler Road to College Counseling Program is here. An admissions officer will review your candidacy at the school of your choice and create a 12+ page personal admission plan. We rate your credentials with the same criteria used by school admissions committees. We assess your strengths and weaknesses and create a plan of action that makes a difference.

Check out **www.collegeprowler.com** or call 1.800.290.2682 for complete details.

# Notes

..................................................................

..................................................................

..................................................................

..................................................................

..................................................................

..................................................................

..................................................................

..................................................................

..................................................................

..................................................................

..................................................................

..................................................................

..................................................................

# Pros and Cons

Still can't figure out if this is the right school for you?
You've already read through this in-depth guide; why not
list the pros and cons? It will really help with narrowing down
your decision and determining whether or not
this school is right for you.

| Pros | Cons |
| --- | --- |
| | |
| | |
| | |
| | |
| | |
| | |
| | |
| | |
| | |
| | |
| | |
| | |
| | |
| | |
| | |

# Notes

..............................................................................

..............................................................................

..............................................................................

..............................................................................

..............................................................................

..............................................................................

..............................................................................

..............................................................................

..............................................................................

..............................................................................

..............................................................................

..............................................................................

..............................................................................

# Notes

........................................................................

........................................................................

........................................................................

........................................................................

........................................................................

........................................................................

........................................................................

........................................................................

........................................................................

........................................................................

........................................................................

........................................................................

........................................................................

# Get Paid To Rep Your City!

## Make money for college!

**Earn cash by telling your friends about College Prowler!**

**Excellent Pay + Incentives + Bonuses**

**Compete with reps across the nation for cash bonuses**

**Gain marketing and communication skills**

**Build your resume and gain work experience for future career opportunities**

**Flexible work hours; make your own schedule**

**Opportunities for advancement**

Contact *sales@collegeprowler.com*
Apply now at **www.collegeprowler.com**

# Notes

......................................................................

......................................................................

......................................................................

......................................................................

......................................................................

......................................................................

......................................................................

......................................................................

......................................................................

......................................................................

......................................................................

......................................................................

......................................................................

# Do You Own A Website?

Would you like to be an affiliate of one of the fastest-growing companies in the publishing industry? Our web affiliates generate a significant income based on customers whom they refer to our website. Start making some cash now! Contact *sales@collegeprowler.com* for more information or call 1.800.290.2682

Apply now at **www.collegeprowler.com**

# Notes

..................................................................
..................................................................
..................................................................
..................................................................
..................................................................
..................................................................
..................................................................
..................................................................
..................................................................
..................................................................
..................................................................
..................................................................
..................................................................

# Notes

......................................................................

......................................................................

......................................................................

......................................................................

......................................................................

......................................................................

......................................................................

......................................................................

......................................................................

......................................................................

......................................................................

......................................................................

......................................................................

......................................................................

# Write For Us!
## *Get Published! Voice Your Opinion.*

Writing a College Prowler guidebook is both fun and rewarding; our open-ended format allows your own creativity free reign. Our writers have been featured in national newspapers and have seen their names in bookstores across the country. Now is your chance to break into the publishing industry with one of the country's fastest-growing publishers!

Apply now at **www.collegeprowler.com**

Contact *editor@collegeprowler.com* or
call 1.800.290.2682 for more details.